Unlocking A More Productive You

DISCOVER THE 3 KEYS TO MAKING SPACE, INCREASING FOCUS & GETTING MORE DONE

Charlie Hugh-Jones

Charlie Hugh-Jones / Unlocking You LLC
West Palm Beach, FL
www.charliehughjones.com

Ordering Information:
Quantity sales. Special discounts are available on quantity purchases by corporations, associations, and others. For details, contact the "Special Sales Department" at the address above.

Unlocking A More Productive You/ Charlie Hugh-Jones Name. — 1st ed.
ISBN 978-0-9994742-0-4

Contents

DEDICATION

"What you get by achieving your goals is not as important as who you become in achieving your goals"

For Samuel and Elayna - I love who you are and who you are becoming

PRAISE FOR CHARLIE HUGH-JONES

"He [Charlie] brings a tremendous strategic perspective that is leveraged with excellent execution perspective. The result is a plan that delivers extraordinary outcomes. I find his insights and perspectives invaluable." Sammy Thomas - CEO, EuroTower

"Working with Charlie is not just fun, it's deeply rewarding - my business is growing, my confidence is increasing and I'm stretching myself to achieve new goals. Most importantly, my spouse and my clients recognize a more empowered, more purposeful me!" Marcella Kiernan - Owner Pilates PBCC

"He [Charlie] is passionate and tireless with his convictions as well as being compassionate and encouraging in his support. He also makes a damn good jogging partner!" Peter Johnson - Founder, JAM Inc.

Foreword

Hello, thanks for picking up my book.

If you ask any professional, high-performer, passionate entrepreneur or business owner what they want more of, the most common response will be to say they want more time!

What I've written in this book will not magically give you more of this most scarce resource.

Instead, I'll show you how to use your time to get more of what you really want.

You see time, like money, is just a tool – and like most tools, it's what you do with them that really count. You can build a small house or a giant skyscraper; you can craft a coracle or construct a supertanker, with the right tools.

Learning how to use a specific tool is one of the most fulfilling things you can do. But putting that tool into the service of something greater - using the tool for a specific end, to achieve a specific goal, not just for its own sake - now that's even more significant. Learning when to use a tool for a specific outcome, learning the strategy, that's the real trick.

True productivity isn't getting more done – it's getting more of what matters most, done. And it's doing that without the stress, overwhelm and anxiety that our hyper-connected, always-on, intensely demanding world provokes in us!

It took me some years and many mistakes to learn the tools and strategies in this book that will give you space to focus, more energy and will ultimately unlock a more productive you.

I didn't set out to be a writer, speaker or coach. I didn't originally plan to become a Life & Business Strategist – I was a musician and an attorney, whose world was governed by 6 Minute Units and whether each unit was productive or not.

If you like stories, then the first half of this book tells part of my story; the Rise and Fall of the 6 Minute King – I'll let you in on how I learned the lessons and paid a heavy price for the principles, tools, and strategies that I use every day. The principles, tools, and strategies that transform the lives and businesses of those whom I have the privilege of working with. The same principles, tools, and strategies that I'm going to give you in the second half of the book.

If you'd rather skip the background and 'cut to the chase', then you can turn straight to the second half of the book. You can dive right into the principles. You can learn the tools and strategies, determine where they fit into your story and put them into practice right away.

Wherever you start, I'm excited for you. I know your time is valuable, but I also know that investing it in reading this book will reward you immensely if you trust the tools and do the work.

(And in case you were wondering, we each have 1440 minutes in our day. That's 240 x 6 Minute Units. Just saying!)

CHAPTER 1

The Contract

Right from the start, I was always trying to do everything at once - even at University - and most of the time I succeeded. Well that's what I thought at any rate. You see "success" is relative – it's relative to the cost you and especially others pay for it!

In reality, however, I was establishing a pattern of behavior that would ultimately be my undoing.

I truly believed I could do everything and have everything at University:

> I arrived at University with the English equivalent of a 4.0 GPA
> I had my own business that gave me more money, freedom and choice than my friends
> I had an attractive and witty Irish girlfriend
> I had my faith and was a respected youth leader in my church

I started a band that later went on the play Richard Branson's 50th Birthday party

I was the first in my year to secure a training contract at a prestigious national law firm

So I figured I looked pretty impressive. To borrow someone else's language – I was a Badass at University!

I believed I could outwork, outsmart and outperform everyone and I could do it while having fun and smiling. That was going to be the key to my success. The results I got from doing things my way seemed to back that up too.

But I was fooling myself. I fooled myself into believing that being manically busy - too busy even for friends - was a good thing.

I fooled myself that being the first to have a mobile phone (they were bricks in the early 90's) - to manage the various events that I was organizing so that everyone but me could have a good time - was cool.

I fooled myself that getting *"there"* quicker than anyone else was going to make me content. And getting *"there"* was the training contract.

You see, it all starts with the training contract. At University, we called it the BMW factor: who was going to be the first to get their BMW? You wouldn't use that now because a BMW's not prestigious enough. It would be the Porsche or Tesla factor or something like that. But for us, at that time, it was the BMW factor.

We were in University, we were supposed to be finding out who we were and enjoying some degrees of freedom but at the same time, when we were in our second year, all we were thinking about, all we could intently focus upon, was...

"the contract"...

The training contract we were going to secure which would position us for success at one of the top law firms.

This, in turn, would then get us on track to work like crazy to the point where we'd finally make partner.

That's the goal. That's how you become this respected, high-functioning professional. That's the top of the pyramid. Making partner is the Holy Grail of the Six Minute Unit. It really is, for most people who set out on a career as a lawyer.

And the first milestone of success was *"the contract"* – and I got there first. I was the first in my year to secure that training contract. This was pretty amazing given that I didn't really want to do law in the first place!

My true passion was music: I'd been playing in bands since I was 14 and the first gig I'd ever played was to over 1000 people. But... and here's the thing... I had a 4.0 GPA out of high-school, and everyone expected me to do something "professional". My high-school tutors and my parents wanted me to become a lawyer.

My high-school was a feeder school for Oxford and Cambridge. (Oxford and Cambridge are the Harvard equivalent in England.) I had the grades and the school had the connections but I quietly rebelled - and I refused to go. This is because, at the time, I believe that the pressures of academic life are going to stop me enjoying music and having fun and building my own business. So I rebel against my parents and rebel against my school, and choose not to go.

Instead, I go and do year a year of Business, Accountancy and Economics at Sheffield University. (This is still a good school; they call it "red-brick" in England and it's the equivalent of an IVY League school.) I end up at Sheffield, rather than Oxford or Cambridge, because my subconscious was telling me something about what was important to me. But I wasn't quite mature enough to hear the subtleties of what it was trying to tell me just yet.

So I did this non-descript business degree because I wanted to run companies. I wanted to grow companies. Perhaps in the music business. But I quickly find out that it's far too easy. It's dull, and if I read a textbook, then I know as much as the tutors who are standing up in front of me. All they seemed to do was recite the textbook. And I can read super quick. So I'm very bored, very quickly.

I get to thinking "Maybe my folks and my high-school tutors were right?" Maybe I should have been doing Law. I'm at a good school, I'm bored, so I might as well do Law anyway. So I transfer into the Law program and get busy doing everything else I wanted to, like setting up my own business.

I made a lot of money at school.

In the English college scene, you have a formal, a ball – a prom - for each specialist school; engineering/medicine/business/ geography/social science/chemistry/materials science, you name it, they had an event. And I became known as the guy who could put together all the people you would need to have an incredible time. I became a promoter while also being a Law major.

So I started and ran a successful business. I was recruiting bands, table magicians, balloon artists, an indoor circus, string quartets, jazz pianists, PA guys, everything you'd need to put on an amazing event. I even found time to start a Motown-style band called "The Great Glass Elevators". (When I stopped playing with them and turned over management to one of the other members, I heard that they had gone on to play Richard Branson's 50th birthday party.) I got up to all kinds of great stuff apart from making friends, hanging out and finding out who I was.

So everyone sees me rushing around looking successful, always with a grin on my face, always exuberant and always full of enthusiasm for life.

What they don't see is me being hospitalized - mid-way through my second year - having suffered a spontaneous pneumothorax. That's when a lung splits in a tiny place and spontaneously deflates. It's a risk factor for super high-performance athletes and mountaineers – not 20-year-old college students. I'm pushing my body so hard, and it is trying to tell me something – but I'm not listening. I just ignore it and move on.

I have everything I think I want and I'm getting *"there"* quicker than anyone else in my year.

At the end of my second year, the recruiters are so impressed with my grades, my extra curricular activities, my attitude and my work ethic, that I manage to secure *"the contract"* before anyone else.

CHAPTER 2

From College to Career

So there are some little clues here. There are some little hooks, some little keys, some life lessons that I was given the opportunity to learn at College - but didn't. I probably should have listened to what God, the Universe, my essential-self, whoever it was, was trying to tell me but I didn't.

I study Law as an undergrad, secure "the contract", and then go to Law school for a year; of course, I passed with commendation. As the kind of guy who goes out there and networks and tells people the future I want to see, and how I'm going to get there, a lot of the law firms liked that. So, when I applied to the law firms and I spent time getting to know the partners and figuring out how I could be seen as an attractive candidate to them, they responded in kind: I was the first person in my year to get "the contract".

For the top firms, you apply for "the contract" halfway through your undergrad degree, even before Law school. So for many of us it was nearly two and a half years before we were actually going to take it up. Imagine that! Your future's set and you have to follow the tramlines to stay on track. And I did it while doing all this other stuff.

The firm I joined was called Nabarro Nathanson. It was the preeminent commercial property firm in England and Wales, based in London. But they also had an office in the North. So I split my time between the northern and southern offices. The reason I really liked them as a firm was because they didn't just do real property - land, office buildings, manufacturing plants - they also did a lot of intellectual property. They did copyright, design right, trade marks, sports rights, etc. And ultimately I wanted to blend my music career and my legal career and be a music attorney. I was doing Law anyway so why not do both? I always thought I could do everything I wanted and all at the same time; it had worked at University so why not in my legal career?

When I joined the Firm, it seemed like "Wow, Charlie gets to do what he used to do,

but now he gets to do it with a suit on. Charlie gets to dress up!" That seemed cool to me: I could be this guy in a band but also this guy in a suit, and I could switch. My father was a very well-dressed gentleman. He wore these beautifully tailored suits, handmade shirts, etc. So I'd already had those kind of things in my world, and now I got to dress the part too.

I loved the fact that I would go into the office, that I'm doing something professional, that I'm getting to use some of my intellect, that I'm working with some of the biggest names in commercial property, developing some of the most prestigious real estate in the

United Kingdom, and that I look the part. And I'm like "This feels good, doesn't it?!"

I sort of play the role and inhabit this character. That's why I say it's dress up. So I began to go "OK, I've been able to run around and study and have a meaningful relationship and run a business all at the same time. So this being paid to be in a Law firm shouldn't be a problem, should it?" And it wasn't. For a while.

I was playing semi-professional rugby. I was playing in a band. I was just married to my university girlfriend. And then half way through my contract, we got pregnant with Samuel, my first son. That's when the way I was doing things began to shake ever so slightly. Almost imperceptibly.

There was the beginning of this shadow inside. The hint of an internal struggle that I barely recognized or acknowledged. "Was this what I actually wanted?"

I was great at being the professional, being the guy who could deliver for his clients, which I proved many, many times even in the training contract. I could outperform most people. There were nearly 40 of us trainees, so it was pretty competitive as there were only 15 - 20 full-time places after the training contract.

It was during this two-year contract that I learned the "6-Minute-Unit": every 6 minutes was monitored, tracked and judged; it was either chargeable to a client, or it wasn't. It either counted, or it didn't. And I could put that Charlie energy and intellect to work and get those units. I could learn the processes quickly. I could deliver for the firm, and I could be great in front of clients.

We had this networking event that was just for young professionals; all the trainees were able to go and network with the trainee accountants (CPA's) and the trainee property developers and the bankers. The rationale was so that we could build relationships and have this network as we all grew up together over our careers. I become the chair of the northern branch so by the time I make partner, I know the senior accountants, commercial bankers and senior partners in the firms we all worked with in the city. And I became the guy who helped host the events and did the networking and went out and began to build these relationships.

Then things shifted when Samuel came along, my first son. Here was this first again – I was the first Dad in my age group – tick, got that box covered – on my way to a happy, successful family.

So now I've added being a father to my accomplishments. But I was like "Oh, don't I want to be home a little bit more often?" Because I was out a lot of the time. Putting in the hours in the office, then putting in the business development hours. Being known as the guy who had the energy and the intellect, not only to get the deal done, but to have fun while we were doing it.

And there are a couple of moments where my then wife, turned around and said, "Whoa, whoa. Could you not.. would you not be out so late ... could you make sure you got home a little earlier?" And I'm like, "hm that's interesting. Yeah, but I want to do this."

And then I found out accidentally, with a complete lack of consciousness ... all my music had disappeared. I suddenly realized that I'd stopped playing. "When did that happen?"

It had happened unconsciously. The momentum, the being celebrated for being a great business developer, and being celebrated for pleasing clients and for hitting the numbers. I began to have these moments suddenly. I didn't listen to them because I didn't learn for another ten years to listen to them but just went, "Whoa. You've lost something that you valued there. You might lose something that's important here." So I lost something of value, my music memories, musicianship and playing in bands and doing that. And perhaps I'm not paying enough attention to Samuel, my newborn son either.

I was still fooling myself that I could do it all – I was overworked, overstretched and lying to myself (ever so subtly) that I can get it all done. That I could be all these things, for everyone I was trying to please, all at once. But maybe the cracks were beginning to show – I just wasn't paying careful enough attention.

CHAPTER 3

New Law Firms & Life Lessons

S o I pass the UK equivalent of the BAR exams and qualify as an attorney. I successfully complete the contract at that firm, and I'm expecting to hit the next milestone – "the offer". Basically, for me, this was to secure a newly qualified role in the technology media and intellectual property group. That way I can get back to my music by practicing law in the music and entertainment business.

I got offered every position apart from that one.

The one thing I wanted. The one thing I'd been working for. The one thing I'd let go of my music for in the first place. The one thing that had prompted me to play a little fast and loose with the family thing to achieve it. That was the one thing I didn't get. There were reasons for it that I wasn't privy to – they were way above my pay grade – but the upshot was, that I didn't get what I'd been working toward for nearly 4 years.

Because I was disappointed, I wanted to get out of there. So I decided to find another law firm.

And I did. I secured an offer from another Magic Circle law firm - one of the top 10 law firms in the UK. The firm wasn't based in London, but it was still one of the preeminent firms. The role they wanted me for was as a newly qualified lawyer in their project finance and banking team.

I'd had this phenomenal mentor - a partner called Mark Rocca - who had spent a lot of time investing in me. He was a project lawyer and thought I'd be great in his team because project law was a little bit of everything. He thought that would keep me engaged and motivated. But I didn't want to stay at the firm that I thought had let me down.

So I'm sitting there thinking "The offer isn't anything like what I want to do. But hey, I enjoyed working with my mentor Mark Rocca. He'd been a project lawyer in London and the Middle East. He'd done all kinds of cool infrastructure stuff; buildings, roads, bridges, power stations, seaports, hospitals, etc. So maybe this might be enough for me, for now."

So I go and talk to Mike, the partner in charge of the project team at the new firm and his right-hand person, a woman called Katherine Ibbotson. She had this phenomenal intellect, an incredibly magnetic personality and was a fantastic mom as well.

This was like, oh interesting. She had a son called Sandy who was exactly the same age as Samuel. And Katherine had this amazing confidence and an attitude that seemed to say "I'm in charge of my life. I'm well respected. I'm brilliant at what I do. But I want to see my son, as well. So that is what I'm going to do."

And that's exactly what she did. I was super interested in that because I'd kind of pulled back on my family time as I thought it was the inevitable cost of climbing the ladder to partnership. But what I saw was that you can be this high profile lawyer – she was acknowledged in the press as one of the top 30 under 30 – and still see your family.

So okay, maybe the role isn't the role I wanted. It's not in the music and entertainment business. But it's project law, so it's sexy, and it's demanding. It's high-profile, and it's lots of money. It's big multi-disciplinary teams, and it's going to be hard work. I can get my head around that and maybe even my enthusiasm too. Perhaps I can do some music and some other stuff on the side? So eventually having considered those criteria, I decided to join them.

Let me tell you this one story though. The final interview was one of the most curious things ever to happen to me. I talk about this regularly now as it is so profound. We often get moments like this popping up in our lives and careers, but at the time I didn't recognize it for what it was. A warning, a red flag, something so prescient and magical for me if I was willing to "get" it. But at that time I didn't have the maturity or consciousness to see it for what it was.

I have a final interview with the head of the banking practice - let's call him Jeremy. I'd already met all the team that wants me to join them, but the final hurdle in the process was an interview with one of the most senior partners in the firm.

Now, this is a firm that's turning over like three hundred million pounds, so nearly five hundred million dollars, half a billion dollars. It's a big firm. So this is a big guy. A guy who regularly takes home a couple of million etc.

During my interview with Jeremy, we get to talking about family. He's asked me why I want to join Katherine and Mike's team, why do I want to do project work. I begin talking about my son, as well as all my accomplishments - which he grills me about - and my interests in music. And he asks me how I'm going to commit, how am I going to make time for all of this. I start talking about the wonder of this new little boy and how I just have to make time for him like Katherine does. And then the weirdest thing happens, he breaks down and cries in my interview. This is the head of banking practice, one of the most senior partners in the firm, one of the highest paid guys. And he cries.

He wells up with tears, and he starts to say something to me in faltering English:

"This morning, Charlie.... you have to keep that. No matter what you do... you have to keep that focus on your son. [sob] just this morning, I walked past the breakfast table where my nine-year-old and my 12-year-old were eating cereal. They pulled me up as my son Matthew turned around and said to me, 'Dad, you haven't a clue who I am. All you do is work. And you come in here, you walk past breakfast, and you walk out the door. You don't know who I am. I wish it was different.'"

Then he just sighs and sits quietly for a few moments, for what seems like an age to me!

I'm stunned. I'm in an interview for one of the highest paid newly qualified jobs in the country and the guy who's interviewing me, the guy who I want to be, a senior partner in a law firm, who has the world at their feet, does international deals, earns loads of money ... he's telling me his son called him out that morning for not being there for him, for not knowing who he was.

Jeremy closes with this - "So Charlie, no matter what you do, if you join this firm, you have to stay connected to your son." - so that's the message I'm supposed to take away, that's the terrific warning the Universe has conspired to give me right at that moment, decision time when I'm trying to impress the person I want to become.

As I said earlier, I get the job offer. That should have been a foundational moment for me. Because the universe has been trying to tell me this. God's been trying to tell me this for the past couple of years ... and there's a risk that I'm going to miss it if I keep going so fast. Even in the interview process to join this massively high performing team, the guy who's interviewing me shows me the very real, very human cost of not staying connected with family while trying to be a high performer.

I get terrific advice from one of the most senior partners. I have an incredible role model in one of my new colleagues. But although I pause momentarily to take this in, it's not long enough to truly internalize the truth, to learn the lesson.

Instead, I rush headlong into the "6-Minute-Unit" driven world of the newly qualified lawyer to make my mark, to make it to the next milestone. A momentum that just keeps building year on year, that all started in College and was reinforced in the training contract. You see, we had accountants come in and show us how profitability in professional service firms works. They lifted the hood, and they showed us the workings and said "This is how leverage works. This is why you have a pyramid with the partner at the top. You have a partner, and then you have a junior partner, then a bunch of senior solicitors, and this is the gearing, and this is how you bill clients, and this is how every "6-Minute-Unit" works for you if you can work it right." That was where the addiction started – where I got hooked on the "6-Minute-Unit".

And over the course of the next three years, I get more and more productive. Better and better at delivering for clients, better at business development and developing new relationships and I suppose I lose myself.

I lose myself to the drug of high-performance and the rewards of my productivity; recognition for targets exceeded in almost every area.

So the first law firm sets the foundation. Then between the two, there's this opportunity where I have this incredibly profound interview process that foretells of who I might become if I don't learn the lesson now. And then at this second firm, I continue along a path barely heeding the warning but becoming successful and getting closer to my ultimate goal faster than those around me – that of becoming a partner.

CHAPTER 4

The Rise and Fall of the 6 Minute King

My day is entirely judged in 6 minute intervals. Every 6 minutes either matters or it doesn't – it either counts or it doesn't – it's either moving me toward my goals or it's not.

And I quickly learn that by harnessing my energy, rigorously structuring my day and prioritizing clients' needs, I can deliver both for my clients and for the firm – I can add value! As I intuitively begin to know how to leverage the systems and processes of a Law firm I also learn how to get noticed and rewarded for doing this really well.

I was studying Allen, Covey, Carnegie, Peters and Maxwell. I was reading Ziegler and Robbins. I was studying all kinds of people to figure out how to be the most effective lawyer. But I was looking at them through the lens of "how does this serve me becoming a partner as quickly as possible, making more money, doing more billable hours than anyone else". That's what I was harnessing it for.

Rather than appreciating the underlying message of all those great writers, which is about the kind of person you can be. I was just trying to use the techniques I wasn't focused as much on the character stuff. So I read lots. I looked at different time management gurus and systems. I learned about my urgent, non-urgent, important, non-important quadrants. And I learned to build priority action models at the beginning of my day that said roughly "Right. I need to achieve this by the end of the day. Here's my 24 hour goal, 48 hour goal, 72 hour goal."

So I started applying these principles to client work and business development. But they spilled over into my recreation. I knew I needed to be relatively healthy to be productive so I was working out. Without really noticing it I started measuring my gym time in "6-Minute-Units" - how much time I spent on the rower and how much time I stretched, how long I spent on the bike. So instead of thinking normally, I started transitioning what I had to do for my firm to bill clients into my gym time.

So when people were say, rowing for 2 and a half or 5 minutes, I was trying to do sequences of 2, 3 a or a full 6, to make up a "6-Minute-Unit". And stretching wasn't 10 minutes, it had to be 12 minutes or 6 minutes. And it just became this operating system for me. And I could see hours in 10 X 6 minute segments.

At the time my wife would be like "We're going to schedule this in with friends." And I was having less and less time for friends, unless it was deliberately scheduled in. There was no spontaneity. It was going to be according to this rigid framework I was working to - this made sure that I got everything done for my clients, but didn't give me much time or much freedom or much spontaneity to just hang out with friends.

My attitude toward socializing began to change too. My thoughts begin to shift to thinking: "Well, these kind of friends are not going to help me move the business along. They're not going to get me new clients." Because many of our friends at the time were local, they weren't in banking or finance in the city or working with one of the big civil engineering firms or mechanical engineering firms, which is what I needed for my business. I began giving them less and less priority. So not only did I start thinking in "6-Minute-Units", I started judging my friendships on whether they were part of my business development effort.

This operating system in my mind - that I had somehow programmed as the way to secure my success, that was going to keep me on track for partnership - was actually mortgaging my time with others. I was fooling myself that this was okay. Building those friendships, around who we were not what jobs we did, could wait. The mantra I kept repeating to myself was that I would do that once I'd made partner, then I could focus on everything else.

I was making some time for my son – I guess some of that lesson from my interview had somehow embedded itself in my subconscious. Other than that, I was myopic. Telling myself that if I don't focus on the "6-Minute-Units", if I don't keep my eye on the prize, the partnership, then I wasn't going to get there. So it's like putting blinkers on. I harnessed tools. I found new ways of learning really quickly with these novel techniques, to cram more into my day, to create prioritization decision-frameworks and criteria, that were very automated in many respects. It made everything black and white.

But it didn't leave any room for spontaneity or shades of grey – which is what real life is like. After a couple of years of doing that, even though I had this fantastic mentor who had tried to coach me in making time for my son, I was still conflicted. I rationalized that it was all right for her, because she's 5 years more senior than me. She's already put in all this groundwork before she had a kid. Allowances were made for her by the partners because she is so amazing and had already proved herself – I was yet to do that, I was still climbing. I've had a son early and I'm trying to get to where she is.

My work ethic, my ability to learn and apply new things quickly and being in a high-performing team was generating results.

I was great at project work and I had great clients. It was intense because you're trying to manage so many moving pieces. Back then we were at a point in time in project finance where a new type of public/private partnership model was being created. And I was one of the most junior people but even so I got to develop some of these sophisticated payment mechanisms for projects that had never been structured this way before. So intellectually I was satisfied, working with phenomenally bright people, doing highly complex tasks.

We sometimes came across as a little more arrogant than the rest of the lawyers around us. Because we had to be masters of lots of stuff. Other lawyers focused on one area and became more specialist by repeating types of work many times in a particular area, say, commercial real estate, planning, structured finance, corporate transactions or private wealth or whatever it is. The project finance team had to be masters of lots of disciplines though – we were expected by our clients to have a much wider perspective and know more and be able to handle more. We were expected by our clients to be this way and we expected it of each other too. But it was an exclusive club – we could do 5 things well, the other lawyers could do 1.

So there was an arrogance that was creeping in to me too. Because our team were the 'top-of-the-top' in the law firm.

About 18 months in, quite out of the blue Katherine turned around one day and said "Charlie, I've been looking at some of the articles you wrote. Would you be happier moving to the Technology, Media and Intellectual Property Team?"

I was surprised and pretty excited. That department did the kind of work that was related to the role I had wanted when I qualified and the copyright laws that applied to music also applied to software in many ways. I had been trying to stay connected to that world through the articles that I wrote and Katherine had spotted this along with the fact that I was gravitating towards the massive technology projects rather than the civil engineering ones.

Katherine had also recalled a single conversation we'd had in the interview process years earlier so asked me a question about it: "Charlie, wasn't one of your aspirations to do intellectual property and music and trademarks and all that kind of thing?" And I'm like, "Yeah, it was, but we've been having a great time. I've learned a lot, maybe this is what I'm supposed to be doing." And she said "You know what? You should be doing project work, but you should be based in the Technology, Media, and Intellectual Property Team."

So Katherine found a very senior Partner to sponsor my move to this other team – keeping one foot in the project team but also allowing me to do some cool technology work too.

And so I moved teams. I'm now sitting with the guy who wrote the new constitution for the Republic of New Zealand. He's just moved to England, he's joined the team. So again, these are high profile lawyers who have done cool things. And I after I've shown that team what I can do and how I relate to new clients, I get nominated to be seconded to our highest profile new client; PricewaterhouseCoopersConsulting.

So this is the law firm's highest profile new client, and one that could potentially become one of the biggest clients. The senior partners want to embed a senior lawyer within that organization to develop business, to grow relationships and to feed work back to the mothership. And they don't want some partner in there, because it's too expensive. They want to put in a senior lawyer, but to them I look like the best candidate for the role even though I was more junior than they were originally considering. They reckon I'm up for the job because they've seen what I can do, how hard I work, how great I am at business development and how broad my skillset is coming from the project team.

So I get nominated to go, to be seconded into the PricewaterhouseCoopersConsulting legal team. My wife at the time, thinks this is a really, really bad idea. For good reason too. I'm going to be commuting from the north of England to London by plane a few days a week. I'm going to be away from her and Samuel a lot of the time. And she really doesn't want to have to pay that cost. And she tells me in no uncertain terms "Charlie, this is not something you should consider. Please don't do it." But I'm thinking, this is the shortcut I've been looking for. This is the opportunity to move ahead quicker than everyone else. This is the fast-track baby!

Because I'm so confident that I can do everything and have everything, because of my ambition and in my arrogance, I say 'yes'.

I say yes even though my wife asks me not to. And I start commuting, getting on a plane at five thirty in the morning to fly down to London and be at my desk at eight thirty. Even before the lawyers in London are at their desks. And the first 6 months of this are brilliant, absolutely fantastic. And the reports are great and they love having someone on the team and the law firm's getting more and more business from PricewaterhouseCoopersConsulting. And I've got great clients internally. I'm working with the oil and gas team. I'm working with the technology team. I'm working with the media teams and Reuters. I'm working with the music team, doing lots of training and they have Elton John and Sting and all these artists as clients. And I'm like;
"Hell yeah, this is as close to rock and roll as lawyering can get!"

And I'm missing out on life back home.

And I'm missing out on the fact that my wife, who is a university lecturer, in academia, is lonely and she's not getting enough attention from me, nor is my son, my Samuel. But I'm getting these accolades for being the guy they picked to launch and be involved in the most important new relationship for the firm. I'm 160% of target. I am absolutely the "6 Minute King" right at that moment. And then something goes wrong.

The partner who was supervising me turns around and says "Charlie, you've done some fantastic work, but we're pulling your secondment because it's just not working, we're not making enough money."

I'm like "How the heck can that be? I was a 160% target." And he responds, essentially saying that I was only 70% of target and that perhaps it had been a mistake to use someone so junior as I just hadn't made them enough money from the secondment. To me that just didn't make sense.

When it was finally unraveled, the story goes that some partner in another department had made a mistake in one of the big litigation suits that they were working on for this client. To try and make amends, that partner writes off hundreds of thousands of dollars worth of chargeable time - mine included! That's how nearly 3 months of my billable work totally disappeared overnight. And at that moment I get my first taste of the cut-throat nature of the partners' lives and the power struggles between their little fiefdoms within a Law firm. Even though I wasn't involved in the mistake, I was at their mercy. I had lost my trophy – my "6-Minute-Units" – with no say.

And I learn abruptly that it doesn't matter how much you've invested, it doesn't matter what you're doing, it doesn't matter how successful you appear, if you are on the wrong team or someone more senior than you needs to cover their ass, then there are bigger things at play, then you are disposable.

I'm left sitting there incredulous, feeling that somebody else's action has completely robbed me of the fruit of my hard-work, the reward for my sacrifice and the sacrifice I asked my family to make, the success that's due to me. And at the same time my wife at home is saying "Charlie, this marriage is going to fall apart if you don't spend more time here with us. And you need to get to know your son."

So what do I do? I rebel against everything. I turn around and I say "You know what? I'm really valuable to this law firm. I'm really valuable to this client. I can pretty much do what I want. You know what I'm going to do? I'm going to get another job offer - so I have one in my pocket - and then I'm going to ask my senior partner to do a four-day week and be part-time. They can either say "no" and I leave for another job or they will say "yes" and I get what I want.

And I did just that. I secure a job offer with the top law firm in New Zealand, across the other side of the world, and then I ask my current firm to go part time. They say "yes" so I stay.

But what happens next shakes me to my core. A traumatic event involving the death of my parents-in-law threatens to tear apart my wider family. My brother-in-law and I have to deal with some things that normal people shouldn't ever have to deal with in life.

I'd just gone part-time and I spend the next couple of months holding that family together. There were four brothers and sisters. And I take everything I've learned about being a professional, about structure and format and being in control and managing emotions and I stand strong for the whole family.

I show them that we can get through. I help make hard decisions. I become this pillar, this rock, that doesn't seem to feel anything. Because I've learned that my professional persona is really, really good at keeping me upright when everybody else is falling over. When everybody can't make decisions, I can. When everyone is falling apart, I won't. So I held the family together – or at least I think I do.

My then wife, who was already feeling betrayed by me for leaving her and going down to London, is now also utterly devastated. And unbeknownst to me she's begun to form a relationship with a co-worker. Someone who can listen to her and can make her laugh, someone who is light-hearted and much more relaxed. Because me, I'm just serious and straight-forward. I didn't know how to be anything else at that point.

And I was keeping it together at work too. I was still delivering for clients. I was still hitting those "6-Minute-Units". Perhaps I wasn't hitting it quite as hard as before the tragedy affected our family. But I am still part-time - 4 days per week - and respected by my clients and co-workers for effectively doing nearly 6 days worth of "6-Minute-Units" in those 4 days!

The next punch also came out of nowhere.

A few months later Elayna our second child, a little girl, is about to be born by Cesarean section. It's a planned C-section to save the potential distress of the labor on an already psychologically at-risk woman, who'd just been through phenomenal trauma. And I get a call from work saying "We know you're on planned parental leave this week and next. We'd like you to think about where you might want to be instead of being at our law firm. We think you probably ought to go and join someone else. We'll pay you three months pay while you do that."

My response is anything but articulate or professional; "What?" I say "Hold on, are you firing me?" And they go "No, no, no, no, no, no, no. We just want you to take your paternity leave to consider whether you'd be best placed at a different kind of law firm." Double speak!

I'm shocked. I've given my soul to earn this position, to earn the trust of clients, to deliver on these "6-Minute-Units" even when my family was going through so much. But the fact is that they believe I was no longer committed to the law firm. They believe my performance is subpar. This is the guy who was 160% of target, until some litigation partner wiped the client's file of more than half of my time! I had the evidence, so I can prove it but it's too late, they've made their decision and if I make too much noise their offer, to pay me while I find another law firm, will be pulled.

I'm stunned. I'm reeling. I have this extended paternity leave with my new daughter, who's just been born. And I'm thinking; "What the F#@%?" Excuse my French there. So, I speak to an Employment Attorney at a big law firm that was my firm's biggest competitor. It turns out that my Law firm was trying to get a merger through, and the other potential firm had asked for some cuts. They were trying to re-engineer the structure of a number of teams, so they could marry them together in defined ratios. And that meant that nine partners and 32 senior lawyers were surplus. So those individuals had to go if the merger was to be pushed through. And I was one of them.

They were taking a risk here that the lawyers they picked to remove, to make the ratios work, wouldn't sue. Because no-one does that, everyone keeps a low profile. They thought that that they could encourage us to leave without fuss then they could save themselves a lot of money and time. I was an easy target, I'd just been through a family trauma and was on paternity leave – I probably wouldn't think straight…and would just accept it. That's what they must have assumed anyway.

You see, in Europe there's no two-weeks notice. We have a lot more protection and if they had had to formally make us redundant it would have cost them a lot of money to pay each of us out and it would have taken a long time to go through the proper process. It can take up to 6 months in some instances. They thought they could save the money and the time and so took a calculated risk.

And they think if they can just get me to choose to go, it'll cost them nothing. It turns out that 13 of us ended up creating a class action against them for wrongful termination and when it comes out, they settle and pay each of us to go away and keep quiet. We had to sign a compromise agreement that keeps us silent if we want to get paid. So we do. But it's been enough time now, past the limitation period, so I can tell you!

To try and get me to choose to leave, they accused me of a number of things; not being committed to the firm, not being effective enough, not being productive enough, being more focused on my family than on my career. Can you believe that – I didn't. No matter who had massaged the numbers to placate an irate client, the original numbers didn't lie and I knew I was still the "6 Minute King".

During the case, it also came out that once I had gone part-time 3 other high-performing male lawyers had asked to go part-time so that they too could spend more time with their young families. That was not the kind of precedent the law firm wanted to set. So they had wanted to make an example of me – not very fair but hey, this is business.

So I end up joining a third, again national but more specialized, Law firm. They'd asked me to join them to build up a new commercial division for them. I know I'm good at that but need to prove it to myself again. And so I throw myself into that. Not part-time. Full time. I'm not going to make that mistake again.

I'm asked to help build a team with a partner from scratch. And so we do. We build this team into a couple of million pounds (dollars) worth of business and we grow the team to 15 people from just the two of us in a couple of years and I finally make partner. I achieve my goal in 10 dramatic years. But at what cost?

You see, mid-way through my time at that firm my wife stops me at home one night and tells me she didn't love me anymore. Perhaps she hadn't for the last couple of years. (Even though we'd had Elayna together!) She wants a divorce and it's because I seem to be just so focused on "6-Minute-Units" and rushing towards partnership. Building my career, not building my family. Paying attention to my clients, not paying attention to my wife.

So I move out, dejected and lost.

I thought being the "6 Minute King" was going to get me what I wanted. Instead I'm floored, because it's actually robbed me of everything that truly mattered. But I didn't realize that until it was gone.

CHAPTER 5

The Ultimate Day

So we're nearly at the point where I have this almost perfect day. My ultimate day:

A day when I get to enjoy being a great dad connecting with my little kids.

A day when I feel purposeful serving my clients with my growing team and I know I'm super productive, getting to finally close a complex deal for one of them.

A day when I feel energized and fulfilled as I get to round off the day playing the hard-rock café with my band and hanging out for the after party. My ultimate day.

But I'm getting ahead of myself here - that doesn't happen for a few months yet.

I've started working in this third law firm, and I'm putting in the hours doing what I do best. Nine months in, the divorce is being finalized. And during that process, I'm trying to work with my new senior partner, to negotiate some flexibility in my schedule.

My argument sort of goes like this: "Look, I'm great at business development, and this is what you hired me for. And I am great at doing new kinds of complex multi-party, multi-stakeholder work, creating new partnerships to help develop all these things around the country. That's exactly what your clients are asking for right now, and I can grow a team to deliver that. But I'm also trying to make sure I see my kids after this divorce – I want to be able to pick them up from nursery and school two days per week. So the price to you of building this new business and me delivering these new clients is not just my salary, it's me being allowed to leave early two days per week to get to my kids."

Miraculously he seems to understand – he thinks it's a WIN:WIN as long as I keep up my end of the bargain - I can leave the office at 4:45 pm on Tuesdays and Thursdays. I can have this family time.

And so I begin to figure out how do I do this – how to connect with my kids, spend time in their world, play with them, affirm that they are loved even though mom and dad live in different houses – I schedule my day, so I can drop them off at school and pick them up and parent them in my own house - I have them around 30% of the time then – one night a week and every other weekend.

And I get to do this while also building my legal practice and my reputation and that of my firm. We're recruiting great talent and brilliant clients and gaining recognition for the novel projects we're doing.

And over time I even reintroduce music into the mix too. I audition for and then end up playing in a band that starts becoming successful.

So 18 months into this new role, it happens. My Ultimate Day. I've designed my world in such a way that it can happen, and it does!

My little ones had woken up in my house (a cottage really), we'd had this lovely breakfast together around my farmhouse kitchen table, and then I dropped the kids off at school and nursery respectively. I'm feeling deeply connected to them as I say goodbye at the gates.

I get to the office and my day is scheduled really well, with no surprises and plenty of margin time to deal with anything unexpected that does come up. I'm able to focus deeply and get so much done with little stress. I do a great day's work, and even though one of my deals is yet to close, I leave relatively early as I have a gig with my band "Mahoney" at the Hard Rock Café that night.

Quite bizarrely I sound-check in my suit. We're headlining, so there's a couple of hours til we're on stage, so I go to the nearby Radisson Edwardian – it's a really nice hotel – get a whisky, open my laptop, ring my clients and then get in touch with the lawyers on the other side. In 90 mins we'd closed the deal.

I get changed into my T-shirt, jeans and flip flops – quite the contrast from the hand-made shoes, tailored suit, custom shirt and Italian tie I'd been wearing moments before – and head back across the road to the Hard Rock Café.

The gig was amazing and totally blew the crowd away, who go wild, and the 'journos' and A&R people seem impressed, and we get some critical acclaim. We also get interest from Chrysalis, one of EMI's development labels. I finish off the paperwork for the deal until two o'clock in the morning and then finally fall asleep.

That was my ultimate day. That was the day I finally felt satisfied when I fell asleep – a sense of contentment, of professional and personal completeness that I'd been chasing after but had never achieved no matter how hard I'd worked previously. That was the day of the Hard Rock Café gig.

CHAPTER 6

My Wake Up Call

So, I have this perfect day, my ultimate day. Okay, it's a great day but how do I repeat it? What had I learned that I could apply again and again to get the same result?

I find that by applying the principles, I'd learned and using my tools and techniques I can get so much more done than everyone else and get to the things that matter to me, not just my clients or my firm.

But there are still some question marks around how I go about what I do.

Professionally it's great. A few months go by with me beginning to repeat that kind of day more consistently – my tools and techniques are working – I have a system. I'm connecting with my kids. I'm playing in the band. I'm a successful lawyer.

Maybe now I can do it all? Maybe now I can have it all?

But I still make a couple of mistakes though, personally. I was performing at such a high-level, my competence was 'up there', but my character hadn't quite caught up. I mess up a couple of new relationships, and if people Google me and get through enough pages, they'll eventually find a newspaper article about my speeding ban too. "NHS Special Advisor Banned for speeding."

You see I was operating so freaking fast, barely catching my breath long enough to appreciate those amazing days, trying to fit so much in, still outperforming my peers but not connecting deeply with people around me other than my kids. My system, my tools, and techniques were enabling me to do more, be more. But occasionally it was still just sheer force of will – myself and others still paying a cost I wasn't counting.

This showed up in my lack of caution driving everywhere super fast. I was still operating on the "6-Minute-Unit"; for the kids, for work, for the band, for friends. I was still operating by those principles. I hadn't yet internalized the value system that ultimately changed me. The authenticity and maturity that has enabled me to find the balance that enables me to focus on the things that truly matter most – I just didn't have that level of discernment or character at that point.

At that time I'm a special advisor to a number of the core organizations in the National Health Service in England – we're in the midst of re-organizing the whole thing – new service models, new governance models, new ways of working together. And I'm right in the middle of it doing my thing. In those days we had email servers that update in a certain point in time, usually overnight, so you had to get documents out before the email servers clicked over and shut down for a couple of hours.

A client had asked for these emergency documents to be sent out in advance of an early meeting the next day. I don't have remote access (seems so long ago!) so I'm racing back from babysitting my kids at my former wife's house, back to the office to get these emails. And I'm just flying. I see them up ahead, but it's too late – out of the darkness on go the blue and red lights. I'm stopped by some very polite, but firm officers.

The older of the two officers turns around and says in a broad Yorkshire accent "Dude, you are an absolute nut case. You are so out of control. It's a quiet night, and it's five past eleven at night, but you are doing near 70 miles an hour in a 30 mile an hour residential zone." Then he goes on to say something so profound. It's never left me. "Nothing is so important that you have the right to risk other people's lives over – your own life is fair game, go find a racetrack and knock yourself out, but this, this is a residential area!"

I needed to slow down and not just on the roads. To help me learn the lesson, I was banned from driving for 28 days. That was a turning point for me. I'd missed so many opportunities to learn vital lessons, but this one landed. This one finally made a difference – I may have been putting local residents' lives at risk, but it also wasn't lost on me that my own kids would have to pay the price if they lost me.

You think your technique is going to get you out of anything. You think you can cram so much into time. And this was something that I'd finally learned.

It's not about just cramming, hustling, putting in more hours than anyone else – shaving minutes and then seconds off tasks that take others much longer. Doing that will only get you so far. It's not about do more, stay up later, live on four and a half hours sleep. Because that's pretty much where I was. It's about knowing what matters most and focusing your energy on that.

So I revisit all my Allen, Covey, Carnegie, Peters and Maxwell. I reflect upon all the systems and processes I'd built and the tools and techniques I was using. I examined what I thought I'd learned from Ziegler and Robbins and I recognized that I'd missed the point. In my headlong rush to make partner I'd hadn't dug deep enough to understand what I truly wanted but even more importantly, who I wanted to be.

My competence was off-the-charts - what I could do was pretty amazing - but my character and my contribution to a wider world… that still needed some work!

CHAPTER 7

Why I do What I do Now

W hat did that wake-up call give me? A significant course correction that ended up with me completely transforming myself and what I did, not just how I went about it.

I'd become pretty much an expert by then. I was an expert in how to manage my time and build client relationships. I was an expert in developing and managing complex multi-agency deals. I was an expert in winning tenders to be on national frameworks for the sexiest work in our space. And I'd had this personal epiphany: about who I was and what drove me. And it made me look at others differently too. And I suppose that was the trigger for what happened next...

We get a call into the office around 8:30 am on the 23rd December. There's a crisis in the health service, and emergency services are about to collapse in our region right before the Christmas Holiday – the busiest few nights of the year. And one of my senior partners goes to this hastily put-together meeting of 27 NHS and private sector organizations and takes me with him.

So all these organizations are supposed to be working together in concert to deliver services. There are 3 commissioners, a number of providers, ambulance services, technology companies, management companies, diagnostics, some run by the government many of them privately held. It's a complex ecosystem of payors and providers who report to different stakeholders.

They are all in this room because urgent care services have gone critical and are about to collapse. One of the organizations that was given the task of coordinating it all was failing but had kept it hidden until it was just about too late.

This group had been convened to fix the problem that was going to blow up in a few short hours. And I'm sitting there supposed to be documenting the solution they are going to come up with and perhaps making a few suggestions. But instead, I sit through the morning watching as they spend hours describing the problem in increasing detail and arguing over who is most to blame – who had missed the warning signs, who should have known better and who was going to lose their job or contract over this. There's no solution in sight.

I might have been a senior lawyer, but I'm the most junior person in the room. I've got a senior partner there who seems to be saying nothing. I've got these CEO's, CFO's and Chief Operating Officers and the Minister of the Health is on the phone with his private secretary attending the meeting, and all these people are doing is blaming each other and raising their voice and getting angry.

And eventually, after about three hours I guess I'd had enough. This is my Jerry McGuire moment, and I stand up in the middle of them all, and I hear myself saying...

"What the hell are you all doing? This is supposed to be an emergency meeting about sorting-out failing urgent care services. You're supposed to be coming up with a plan, so they don't fail tonight. You're supposed to be making sure that when people turn up to an urgent care center or ER tonight or call the equivalent of 911, they will actually get through to someone! That they will be taken care of! I've got neighbors and friends who will be affected by this, what if they're having a heart attack or having a stroke? What about my kids? And all you're doing right now is figuring out who is the most to blame. These are the kinds of conversations I have with my kids, with the kids I teach in Sunday school, with my nephews and nieces."

The room goes silent. I can see that a couple of the most senior guys are offended and I reckon they're thinking "Who the hell is this?" But then someone else says: "So what do you think we should do about it? What do you recommend?"

And that's it right there. My moment.

So I stand in the middle of this room, and over the course of the next 5 hours, I shepherd these organizational leaders into a deal. I'm focused on a solution, albeit a temporary one ... so that ambulances will turn up the following day, so the ER's know where people are coming from and can coordinate so that the call lines would still be available when people dialed the number. And I'm the center of it.

And I get a lot of accolades. And within a month my firm has offered me a partnership.

I'd made partner. I should have been happy. I've made partner in a law firm almost exactly 10 years from the date I set out on my 10-year plan. I have achieved everything I thought I wanted.

And I was unhappy, desperately unhappy. Even though I'd been having these almost perfect days. I had my kids – some of the time. I had acclaim and recognition - we'd made the front page of the Times! I was doing some intellectually stimulating work. I still worked with the band. And I had made partner. And I was unhappy, desperately unhappy. I had nobody to share it with, other than myself. I was no longer married, I hadn't managed to maintain a relationship. And so when my kids weren't there, I was alone. I hadn't made time for friends. I'd achieved the one goal that was supposed to make all the sacrifices worth while.

So I decided at that point, I needed to do something about it.

I had just been awakened to the fact that these CEO's, CFO's, these Operating Officers, these high functioning individuals, who were paid an awful lot of money to head up these government and private organizations, I realized that they had shown up with fear and insecurity. Their professionalism wasn't enough to manage their emotions in those moments – they hadn't been the best version of themselves when it counted most.

So I started learning about attitudes and behaviors. The values and beliefs that get thrown up in different circumstances and drive decisions. The mindsets and blueprints to trigger how people operate. And that was the beginning of my journey exploring the tools and strategies that would help others Unlock the Best Version of themselves.

Intuitively on that day, I'd used some of tools and techniques that had worked for me, but now I felt compelled to figure out what would work for other professionals. I felt drawn to figuring out what would work at an organizational level, in teams. I realized that this was more important to me than being a partner in a Law firm. I wanted to help individuals and organizations Unlock the Best Version of Themselves. So I made a decision...

I was only a partner for 9 months before I resigned and set up my first business doing just that: Helping individuals and organizations clarify their goals, develop effective strategies to meet their objectives and then take positive action to deliver on them.

I knew I had found my purpose. The fingerprints had been all over my professional and personal life to date, I just hadn't spotted them until now. It was like a weight had been lifted and I felt a deep sense of satisfaction, a contentment that I had briefly glimpsed but had never stayed long.

And that is why I do what I do now.

CHAPTER 8

The 3 Keys

Time to Invest in You

I feel like you might know me a bit better by now – I know that you've invested a considerable amount of your time reading this book if you have gotten to this point. So, I'm going to invest in you too. I'm going to give you the three core principles that Unlocked a More Productive Me, my 3 Keys.

Overwhelm, Confusion & Conflict, Busy-being-busy

If you're a high-performer or passionate entrepreneur like many of my clients, you're probably aware enough to recognize the mode you're in even if you don't admit it to many people.

Sometimes you suffer overwhelm - there's just too much to do and not enough of you to go around. Everything is coming at you all at once, and it doesn't seem to let up. Every single thing demands equal attention, and you're in danger of exhaustion because of your over-commitment.

Sometimes you might have so many thoughts and ideas or so many opportunities staring right at you that making a decision between them seems almost impossible. You are confused or conflicted as to what to do first. So you either try and do everything or you're stuck, and you procrastinate.

Sometimes you spend a lot of time trying to get organized about the million things that need to get done. You get into the weeds and get so busy doing a lot of things that may not be that important. You become a micro-manager and never seem to get back to 30,000ft to get the strategic perspective to work on your clients or your business.

The results can be painful:
Long hours at work
Being overlooked for promotion
Financial trouble
Health problems
Relationship issues
Missed Deadlines
Clients going elsewhere.

And all that creates stress.

If that's you sometimes, then I'd hazard a guess that you blame the stress on a lack of time.

"If I could just have 2 more hours in my day!" – "All I need is more time!"

But if you got two more hours, if you got more time, as I've found with most of my clients, you'd just have more hours of

Overwhelm or Confusion & Conflict. You'd fill that time with being busy.

All you really need...

The issue is not more time – the real issue is space to focus, energy to get things done and a system to make sure it happens consistently.

Understanding and applying these 3 core principles, these 3 Keys, is all you really need to Unlock a More Productive You – to create more space to focus, to have more energy to get things done and to develop a system to make sure it happens consistently.

And these 3 core principles work regardless of the ferocious speed of change in our world, the complexity of business, the increasing expectations of clients and the demands of our connected lives. Developing your own system, based on these 3 core principles, is enough to enable you to manage it all.

It's not about:
A new app or device;
A new, more elegant planner; or
A new piece of software or platform.

These are good tools, and I can recommend many of them that work for me and my clients. But good tools are only useful to the extent you use them to apply these 3 core principles.

These core principles are essential foundations for anyone I work with in my seminars, in my one-to-one coaching sessions, and in my masterclasses.

I'm ok right now

Maybe everything is going just fine for you right now. Perhaps some part of you feels that it's just not that bad. You're organized, you've got a good job, you've got money. Why do you need to Unlock a More Productive You?

From the 1000's of people I've worked with over the years, I'm here to tell you that it can be a whole lot better.

Just how sustainable is your current work and lifestyle in the long run?

How available are you to all kinds of things that are going to come up in a world that is in constant change?

How available are you to family and friends? What capacity do you have to deal with unexpected events?

What bandwidth do you have to take advantage of these opportunities rather than be at the mercy of crises?

It could be a whole lot better.

When was the last time you made space to reflect upon what "a whole lot better" might look like for you? Perhaps now is the time to do that and see just how amazing your life could be.

Why, What, How

So, in the next three chapters, I'm going to share with you these 3 core principles, my 3 Keys.

First I'm going to explain why I know they're critical, why these 3 core principles are so vital to becoming more productive.

Then I'm going to show what it looks like to apply them with examples from my own world.

Finally, I'm going to give you some how's, some tools to apply them in your world so you can begin building your own system and getting results straight away.

Once you get the principles, trust the tools and apply them you will Unlock a More Productive You!

CHAPTER 9

The Power of 'NO'

Creating space to Focus

Why is this Principle important?

Everybody has an agenda for you — if you don't have your own, you will be pulled in every direction under the sun.

Everybody wants something from you: your time, your attention, your intellect and your money. And unless you have your own design, your own plan to keep you on course, you will end up broke, obese and very depressed, let's be honest, because everyone's trying to sell you something.

There is so much input, opportunity, distraction, and demand, in your world:

- there is so much information to process,
- there are so many opportunities to chase down,
- there are targets you have to hit,
- there are distractions that want to steal your time; and

- there are demands that are placed upon you by family, friends, investors, employees, direct reports, business partners, clients and so on.

And not having a plan, not having a framework for decisions around your real priorities, not having a rationale for saying 'no' with confidence and with real conviction, means you're exposed to everybody else's agenda shaping your agenda and robbing you of the space to focus.

The power of 'no' is already in your DNA

Your central nervous system, your whole body, is built to take in millions and millions and millions of sensory experiences every second. Your entire brain is wired with over 100 trillion connections, billions of neurons designed to process millions of bits of data every nano-second.

Your sense of touch processes the temperature over every skin pore on the body every moment.

Your sense of sight processes the billions of photons that are coming through our eyes.

Your sense of smell processes the myriad and plethora of smells that are going in our nostrils at any moment in time.

Your sense of taste is processing the taste of the air; and

Your sense of hearing is processing the thousands upon thousands of sound waves that are at any point in time coming into our ears.

We are always on; we are never off. But our mind finds a way to automatically sift through all that data and only focus on what matters most. By doing so, it helps us avoid the overload that might overwhelm and or distract us.

Your mind already has the power of 'no' built into it unconsciously. You now need to learn how to consciously use the power of 'no' to focus on the things that matter to us most not just our DNA!

You have one job!

Warren Buffett once said that his only job was to say "no". I heard him explain how a thousand investment theses cross his desk every day and his singular focus and role was to say, "no" repeatedly, perhaps 1000 times, until he finally got to something he was compelled to say "yes" to.

Now, it's easy to tell that story and take it lightly until you understand how Warren Buffett does that. He doesn't simply say "no". He applies very specific criteria to an investment thesis, criteria that he has developed over the years.

When I heard that, I knew that I had to figure out the basis for my 'no'. What framework was I going to use in order to shape what I said 'no' to, what criteria would I use to determine my priorities so that I could get to the things that were most important to me, my 'yes'. What was I going to give my time and attention to and what should I be saying "no" to? How would I create space to focus?

I recognized early on that this would define me and what I was able to achieve as a project attorney, given I had so many competing priorities.

Tactics or Strategy?

You see we can use our 'no' tactically and we can use our 'no' strategically. We can manage the "load" of our day, and we can also manage the course of our life.

Tactically, we might want to use our 'no' to avoid burning out or falling over - something's coming at us, we know we're already too busy, and we say "no" because we just can't do any more right now. That's tactical; it's like a circuit breaker. We can use our 'no' so that we don't overload ourselves in the present moment.

Strategically, we can use our 'no' to keep us on course for a longer journey. We have already chosen where we want to get to. To get there, we have to avoid detours and distraction; we have to be able to focus, not to be pulled off course.

Many of my clients are pretty confident in using their tactical 'no' to manage their day. But they come to me because they still don't manage to get to the things that matter most to them. Regularly they feel like they are not moving fast enough, in life or in their business, towards the things that they really want.

Many solopreneurs and small business owners feel the weight of having so many mini-goals or projects, of wearing many hats, of doing multiple roles. They are regularly confused or conflicted about what to do in what order and eventually become exhausted and frustrated!

Many professionals and executives perceive risk in saying "no" to their team, of letting down customers, of alienating potential clients. These are all very real fears, but they lead to negative behaviors.

Too often their 'no' is finally only expressed in crisis. The fear then manifests itself as the thing they were worried about in the first place because the team member, the customer, the client senses the desperation and is repelled by it and usually reacts badly – thus reinforcing the sub-optimal behavior that led to it.

The fact is that this frustration, exhaustion and fear can all be relieved or avoided by adopting the principle of the Power of 'No' to create space to focus.

Where I learned the Principle

I learned the principle behind the Power of 'No' when I was a young attorney working in a top law firm. My success was determined by doing chargeable tasks. I knew as many as possible of my 6-Minutes-Units needed to be filled with stuff that was chargeable to a client. Not only was I up against the clock on a daily basis, I was competing with the best attorneys in my own firm on that track to partnership. I was also competing with other magic circle law firms who were always prowling around ready to pounce on a client who felt the least bit dissatisfied or did not feel that they were our priority!

So, to succeed I needed to figure out how to be insanely productive to make every 6-Minute-Unit count; to say "no" to things that did not count and to create space to focus.

The 'Tax' of Context Switching

Although I understood it intuitively, I didn't learn till much later on that there is a principle called "Context Switching" which is very deeply researched, particularly in the technology sector. It's a very measured approach to understanding the exact loss, the 'tax', on our productivity from switching between tasks.

I needed to avoid switching tasks because there was such a cost to it. Not only did the time wasted compound and make my days longer, it was also really hard to justify small chunks of time to a client.

Every day I meet a lot of great people putting in a lot of effort – but after talking to them I know that their effort isn't being rewarded because they are losing up to 80% of their effort to Context Switching. Back then I was too, until I figured out what to do about it.

I knew that I needed to try and do one thing at a time and where possible create blocks of associated activities to make sure I got jobs done. To do that I had to figure out a system that enabled me to say "no".

So I experimented every day – trying different ways of blocking out distractions, delaying responding to emails, using voicemail more effectively. It was like finding ways of putting blinkers on, like a race-horse, so that I would remain focused on the task at hand.

So, that was how I began developing my own system for saying "no" to interruptions, a system and a set of criteria in order to make sure I could deliver for my clients – of staying on task, of doing one thing until it was finished. I developed a system for my schedule designed to say "no" to activities that sapped my focus, distracted me or just weren't productive.

It's not just 'No' to activities, it's 'No' to people too
But sometimes that 'no' needed to be said face to face or on the phone to a supervisor, to a partner or worse still to a client – and that was hard because I worried what they would think of me. There was risk attached to doing that.

So I decided to figure that out too – how to say "no" in a way that retained trust and retained loyalty: Trust that I would still get a job done for a client and loyalty that they didn't need to go elsewhere – the environment was so competitive, so cut-throat that this was super important to master.

Is your 'no' a WIN:WIN negotiation?

As a lawyer I was studying negotiation all the time: Not just convincing someone you were right or your perspective was correct but how to understand another's point of view, to find out what they really wanted. We were trying to find and use the best tools for making sure deals got done quickly rather than getting hijacked by egos and positions.

My go-to guy was the Harvard-based negotiating guru, William Ury. I'd read his first book called "Getting to Yes!". Some of the principles in it and in some of his subsequent articles became his more recent book: "The Power of a Positive No."

It wasn't about time management or productivity, but it was about getting what you wanted without alienating someone else. His research had shown that a 'positive no' is comprised of three parts. William Ury put it like this:

"Your 'No' has to be a positive No. That means:

1.   It starts with a 'yes' to what is truly important to you – what are your keys interests, your key priorities in a situation; then

2.   It is followed by your 'No', said respectfully and demonstrating an awareness of the impact of the 'no' on the other party; and then

3.   It finishes with a 'Yes', framing a constructive, positive proposal.

e.g., Your boss is asking you to work this weekend – "Yes to the very important family event this weekend – No, I can't work this weekend – and Yes, here's what I can do, I can work late Tuesday night, and I can get John and Mary to help out."

What did my 'positive no' look like?

Given the long hours culture in a city law firm this had a very practical application for me as a young lawyer: Back then I was absolutely killing it by becoming fantastically productive, and clients wanted to work with me. I'm doing project work that was often 24/7, but ultimately I wanted to spend time with my baby son.

(This is one of the relationships I got right and have maintained ever since. I'm really proud of the connection I now have with my 18-year-old son, and I had to say a lot of "No's" to maintain that throughout my career.)

My colleagues and almost everybody else were working stupid hours, staying really late in the office because they were scared to leave. We all thought that if we were seen to leave early, we were not going to get promoted, we'd never be recognized enough to make partner. If we left early, we wouldn't be able to deliver for our demanding clients, etc. But I had this mentor called Katherine, who had a son, Sandy, the same age as my Samuel. She was known as one of the top 30 under 30. She's a brilliant thinker; she was a great lawyer, she had a lot of acclaim for doing the kind of project work we did, which meant she was highly visible.

She basically said to me, "Look, I go home to have tea with my son, to do his bath time, then put him to bed. Then I do more work if I need to. That doesn't have to be in the office. Why don't you try it, Charlie?"

That was it, that was a positive 'no' in action. I was not going to behave like all my other junior lawyers and just stay late and then get home around 9 pm, grab a beer, put my feet up and watch TV. No. What was more important than that, to me, was seeing Samuel. He was my 'Yes'.

So, I learned to manage client expectations. If I was asked to deliver a report or advice by, say, 6:45 pm I'd be bold enough to challenge the deadline to find out when they truly needed the advice or report or whatever. Unless it was specifically to submit a report to regulatory authorities or to complete a transaction, the deadline was usually pretty arbitrary.

So after a while I'd find myself saying, "No, I'm not going to send you that report by 6:45 pm". Because, for example I'd understood from my gentle probing that the decision they were going to make - based upon my advice - wasn't going to be made until a board meeting at 9:30am tomorrow. So I would say instead, "Look, I can get the report to you at 10:00pm tonight" or "I can get the report to you by 5:00 a.m. or 6:00 a.m. tomorrow morning, but I'm not going to get it to you by 6:45 tonight." So there's my 'no', there's my boundary. And it worked.

Building Trust

Gradually clients began to understand this, and the reason I got known for delivering for my clients was because there was no BS from me, there was no bravado. I wasn't trying to look like this high performance lawyer who was always in the office just for appearances sake. Instead I was actually delivering what the clients needed when they needed it and being real about it. I didn't miss deadlines because I grew confident in challenging them.

Now and again it meant I had to break my own rule, but my 'no' always came from a 'yes', to Samuel. My firm 'no', was to avoid working for no reason between 5:45pm and 7:45pm just for the sake of it, just because everyone else did.

I didn't keep a jacket on the back of my chair so I'd look like I was in the office late every night like many of the other junior lawyers. And I worked really hard to find a 'yes' that a client would accept so that that client got what they needed, when they really needed it, and I could still spend time with my son. It was a WIN:WIN - I delivered for my clients and my clients didn't challenge my bills because of that.

Mastering my schedule and my relationships with clients enabled me to find the space to focus on what mattered most to me – delivering for my clients and spending time with my son. For some reason I also seemed to have more fun than the other junior lawyers, perhaps it was because I was less stressed than they were?

Now I regularly find myself reminding my clients of this truth: You can do anything but you can't do everything!

To get to the most important things in your world you need to exercise the power of 'no'.

As I said at the beginning, other organizations have an agenda for you to sell you something, to get something from you. You have colleagues and co-workers who need your attention to help with that project, or to work late, or to finish that report. If you're a small business owner or you're an entrepreneur, you are trying to be the captain of the ship, the navigator, the engineer, the dock master, you try and do all these things at once, and each part of that business is demanding your attention and you need to figure out how you judiciously and deliberately deploy your 'no' in order to create space to focus.

APPLICATION

How to apply the Power of 'No' to create more space to focus

Figure out your 'yes'

Your 'yes' should be a reflection of your priorities, the things that really matter to you. The things that are worth saying "no" to in order to have. These might be short term or long term – what do I want/need to do now or what do I want/need to achieve longer term - they can be tactical or strategic goals.

You may already have a good idea of what they are. If so, you might just need a clearer picture of what you are doing or not doing that slows you down or doesn't help you get there. If that's you then skip on to Tool 3 to get a better handle on your habits and behaviors.

If not, then here's a quick way to determine what goals are really important to you both professionally and personally.

Tool 1 – Determining what goals matter most to you

Professionally - Write next year's performance review

Step 1 - Try to imagine that you're coming up to your performance review next year.

Step 2 - Ask yourself this question: What 3-5 things will be mentioned in your performance review that will have made it a great year for you?

Step 3 - Write down that list

Personally - Write next year's holiday letter

Step 1 - Try to imagine that it's coming up to the holiday season next year and you're writing your holiday letter to friends and family.

Step 2 - Ask yourself this question: What 3-5 things will have made it a great year for you and your family that you want to be able to tell others?

Step 3 - Write down that list.

From those two exercises you should have come up with a list of 6-10 goals for the next year. These comprise your 'yes', at least for the next 12 months.

If Tool 1 doesn't work for you, then alternatively why not try this next tool instead.

Tool 2 – Reflecting on what matters most to you

Step 1 - Imagine you are in a circle with 3-5 of you best friends or closest family, people who you trust, who accept you and won't judge you.

Step 2 - Now try and answer the following questions as if they had asked them of you:

- What do you really want out of life?
- What do you value?
- What do you stand for?
- Where are you headed?
- What gives you energy and fulfillment?
- What makes you feel alive?
- What makes you feel connected to others?
- What triggers your ambition?
- What inspires you?
- What circumstance or situation will tell you that you are successful?
- What do you want people to say about you?
- How do you want to be remembered?

Step 3 - Ok, so now you have probably have a list of things for each of the questions you answered. The next step is to put them in rank order. So, for example if you have a list of 5 answers to the question "What triggers your ambition?" try and put them in relative order from 1 – 5.

This begins to give you an idea of the things that matter most to you right now and what you want to say "yes" to.

Identifying the habits and behaviors that don't serve your 'yes'

Now you need to identify the patterns in your behavior that get in the way of you taking action that moves you toward what you really want, what truly matters to you.

You control you, not time and not other people. You are in charge of your 'no'. So you need to figure where to apply it to yourself before you apply it to others.

There's a well-known management maxim that "you can't manage what you don't monitor". The same is true with our own behavior.

Tracking your own behavior is a good way to shed some light on how you spend your time. This in turn will show you where you need to make better choices about what you say "yes" to but instead deserve your 'no'.

I am constantly surprised at just how little people understand about how they spend their day. I'm also surprised at how under-utilized this simple tool is. The self-knowledge it provides and the revelation it provides typically inspires clients to make changes even before I suggest them! They just haven't tried it. The tool comes from the traditional auditors' role in conducting time and motion studies of the 1960's.

Although there are plenty of apps now to help you do this I prefer the old school pen and paper method – it triggers a different part of your brain than when you type.

Tool - 3 Establishing how you really spend your time

Step 1 – Log your activity. So start with a single day, and just observe and note every time you do something like:

- switch activity
- stop for a thought
- are interrupted by a call
- check your phone
- respond to a message
- write a paragraph of a report
- complete a spreadsheet
- grab something to eat
- watch a tv show etc.

Don't judge any action or train of thought, just make a note of it, for a full day - from when you wake up to when you go to bed. Then put it away, you can analyze it tomorrow. The first time you do it will seem awkward and cumbersome but it is so worth it. You then need to make time to analyze it.

Step 2 – Analyze your activity. You can do that by using the following questions:

- What did you notice?

- What did you learn about yourself?
- What habit did you recognize that you didn't realize you had before?
- What patterns emerge?
- How long does it take to get out of the house in the morning?
- How much time do you spend on different activities?
- How frequently do you come back to an activity that you were interrupted or distracted from?
- How many people do you talk to in a day?
- How many times do you check facebook?
- How long do you leave a message before you respond?
- What takes up the majority of your day?
- Which of your activities do you begin to judge now that you see them?
- What might you begin to rearrange?

From the answers to these questions, you'll begin to notice the things you say "yes" to, but which might actually deserve your 'no'. If you've followed through and used Tool 1 or Tool 2 to define what you truly want, then where you ought to be saying "no" will become clear pretty quickly.

Saying "no"

This seems obvious but it is common sense that is not so commonly practiced. Now you have to actually make decisions and say "no".

Now you know what matters to you and you have a rough idea of how you are spending your time. What you need to do next is take action.

Tool 4 - Making 'no' a daily practice

You can do by asking yourself these two questions at the start of each day:

- How can I plan to make space to focus today given what I know now?
- Which activities, interruptions, behavior or patterns am I going to say 'no' to today?

You'll need to determine your own criteria based upon the answers you discovered using Tool 1 and Tool 2.

In the next two chapters I'll share with you the principles, tools and strategies you can use to implement the power of your 'no' to create space to focus. In the next chapter we'll explore why and how you need to manage your energy and then in the chapter after that I'll show you how to create a system to ensure you implement these consistently.

The most effective 'no' to Unlock a More Productive You!

The most common behavior most of my clients adjust when they finally acknowledge it, is around social media, email and messages. Saying no to the distraction of your phone, your messages and social media is the single most effective 'no' you can deploy right away to see immediate results.

When you look at most high performers, successful entrepreneurs and high functioning business execs, their level of planned neglect of social media, email and messages is phenomenal. Their 'no' is pretty strong. And this is something I practice rigorously myself too – it's what helped me write this book in just a few weeks.

So why not batch the time you spend doing this and schedule specific intervals in your day to do it? The same for returning phone calls – is the car the best place to make those calls either on the way into work or on the way home?

In addition, typically you'll find that most high performers don't check their messages for the first 90 minutes of the day. If you open those emails straight away, you are giving power to circumstances that are not in your world yet.

It is very rare for anybody in any business to get an email in the morning regarding something that happened overnight, that someone is going to die if they don't deal with it in the first five minutes when they wake up. But so often our entire nervous system, our fight or flight mechanism is triggered like a Pavlov dog reaction by our phone in the morning. Most people reach for their phone before they reach to kiss their partner in the morning (if you have a partner). I'll talk more about this in the next chapter concerning managing energy.

In the meantime, I'll close with this; if you take nothing else away from this chapter if you don't use the tools and ask yourself the questions I gave you, at least try this:

Track your social media, email and message habits and make one change and see what happens!

CHAPTER 10

Don't Manage Time, Manage Your Energy

Unleashing more energy to get things done

1440 minutes each day – that's how many we are each given.

Edison, Einstein, Churchill, Ghandi, Branson, Jobs, Musk, Elizabeth I, Marie Curie, Mother Teresa, Ruth Bader-Ginsberg, Malala Yousafzi, you and me – we have all been given the same amount of time in our day.

With the possible exception of Einstein, no one in their right mind is going to tell you that if you somehow manage time well, you are going to take 5 minutes and make it 6! The phrase "time management" is so misleading, we can't.

So why do we try?

Like many professionals, initially, my response to a high workload and high-demand was to work more hours. I regularly felt exhausted and found it difficult to engage with my family, which often left me feeling guilty and dissatisfied – and because I didn't learn the lesson quickly enough it also ultimately led to me losing the family life I so wanted.

And that's what a lot of high-performers and passionate entrepreneurs do too, they work 12-14hr days and pay a price they haven't budgeted for. This inevitably takes its toll physically, mentally and emotionally.

I might have been able to outperform my peers and push harder than others, but essentially I was playing a zero-sum game with time. A game that I was ultimately going to lose. As I found out to my detriment, the fundamental problem with working longer hours is that time is a finite resource.

Now energy, on the other hand, is a different story. Energy is a measure of capacity, and for human beings, this energy comes from 3 main wellsprings:

The Body
The Mind
The Spirit

Energy can be depleted, it can be renewed, and it can be expanded. So now I manage my energy and not my time. And when my clients recognize the cost of their own energy depleting behaviors, I help them use tools and strategies to renew and expand their energy in these three areas to become incredibly productive and fulfilled.

It took me nearly 15 years to fully figure this out and master a range of tools and strategies that are effective in each area, but the concept began to take root soon after university.

Not all Time is created equal

It was early on in my career that I recognized that time wasn't the same for everyone. Remember the 6-Minute-Unit? Well, what we charged a client for my 6-Minute-Unit when I was a Trainee was a lot less than for a Qualified Attorney, which was a lot less than for a Senior Attorney, which was a lot less than for a Partner's 6-Minute-Unit. There was a good reason for that!

A Partner might be able to look at a problem and intuitively know a solution, construct some skeleton advice, and report to a client in 12 minutes flat - two units. A Trainee might spend half a day, three and a half to four hours, researching, trying to figure out possible solutions, constructing the best way to structure that advice and then still have to put it in front of the partner for sign off on it.

What a Trainee could do in 12 minutes – two units – was so much less valuable to the client than what a Partner could do in two units. This highlighted to me that some people can do more in the same amount of time as others. Initially, I only understood this regarding a technical subject or expertise, but it is true for creativity, for inspiration, for recognizing a connection with someone that leads to new actions that move the needle.

How much of you is showing up to practice?

There is no shortcut to mastering a technical subject. Please don't get me wrong here. You can't learn to be a master viola or cello player without doing an intense amount of practice. However, you need to do a very specific sort of practice referred to as "deliberate practice" which involves constantly pushing oneself beyond one's comfort zone, following training activities designed by an expert to develop specific abilities, and using feedback to identify weaknesses and work on them.

It is not simply a matter of investing 10,000hrs in repeating an activity. Rather it is a matter of a specific type of focus, leveraging a specific kind of mental capacity to grow, increasing how much of you shows up to practice, the kind and amount of energy you bring to it.

I'm not saying that there aren't techniques to accelerate learning, expert hacks that enable you to learn faster. What I am saying is your ability to learn within that average is completely determined by the state you are in, physically, mentally and emotionally when you show up.

So I began training my mind, to learn more quickly, to push myself out of my comfort zones. These were mental techniques to increase my expertise and concentration so that I could write reports and advice more quickly so that I could identify pertinent issues rapidly, so I could draft massive documents without losing attention to detail. This training helped manage my intellect, but it was a while before I learned how to manage my thoughts as well. And what I found when I did was my greatest step-change in productivity.

Sub-optimal decision-making

One of the most poignant moments in recognizing the power of this core principle was the crisis I helped avert that accelerated me becoming a partner.

I clearly remember standing in the middle of this complete mess and chaos of a potential service failure. It felt like it was inevitable, it was going to fail that night, 23rd of December. We had 27 organizations represented in the room, and everybody is yelling, and it's like a schoolyard, it's like recess when all the kids are angry, and they've been fed too much sugar. These executives were operating from fear and insecurity and from "positions" that were supposed to show strength and not expose weakness or vulnerability. The true interests of their organizations and their stakeholders - what we really needed to achieve to make sure service users could still access services - was being drowned out by this negative behavior.

What I later came to realize was that what I had observed was that when people showed up with the wrong mindset, with the wrong emotional framework, they didn't get anything done or at the very least it took so much longer. They spent hours just defining a problem, rather than solving it. They couldn't be productive. They weren't able to create options to consider and solutions to explore. And that frustrated the living daylights out of me. It's what prompted me to risk my professional reputation by losing standing up and blurting out; "What the f%#* are you all doing? You're supposed to be solving this problem. You're all super clever, you're all really well paid, but you're not helping us solve this."

From that point on, I determined to learn what was going on for people, what impacted their ability to manage their emotions? What impacted their attitudes and behaviors? Why might people show up and display more of their fear-based behaviors than their hope-based behaviors; behaviors that were self-defeating when it came to optimal decision-making.

So let's take a brief look at each of the three wellsprings of energy.

The Body - Physical Energy

I don't think you'll find it a novel idea or a great revelation that inadequate nutrition, exercise, sleep, and rest diminish people's basic energy levels, as well as their ability to manage their emotions and focus their attention.

However, the reality is that many high-performers and passionate entrepreneurs don't find ways to practice these consistently healthy behaviors, given all the other demands in their lives. Instead, they're doing things such as skipping breakfast, failing to express appreciation to others, struggling to focus on one thing at a time, or spending too little time on activities that give them a sense of purpose.

While my clients are never surprised to learn how counter-productive these types of behavior are, when they begin to see the patterns in their own behavior it often galvanizes them into action to change a few of them.

The Mind - Mental Energy

How long does it take to have a creative idea? Zero Time
How long does it take to be inspired? Zero Time

How long does it take to recognize an opportunity? Zero Time

How long does it take to connect with someone who might be your most significant hire who can truly move the needle? Zero Time.

The Battle for Bandwidth

Time is not the issue – headspace is. You need room to think. Room to be creative. Room to be innovative. If you don't have this mental energy to focus, if you don't have this mental bandwidth, then gaining more time will not get you closer to things that matter most. You'll just fill it with more busy-ness.

For me, it was easy to focus when I was first a trainee, but as life became more complex, as family concerns grew when children arrived and I became more senior, the battle for my attention grew immensely.

Our always-on, hyper-connected world of FOMO and increasing corporate anxiety has multiplied this demand for our attention exponentially. The constant stream of emails, texts, and social media posts blurs our focus to the extent we let it.

Cal Newport, professor at Georgetown and author of "Deep Work Rules for focused success in a Distracted World", thinks the ability to stay focused will be the superpower of the 21st Century.

"Those who can sit, undistracted for hours, becoming masters of their subjects, creating things that the rest of us choose to use will rule the world – while the rest of us frantically and futilely try to keep up with texts, tweets, and other incessant interruptions." Sounds like a clarion call for applying the power of no!

We don't just need to avoid distraction though; we need to increase concentration. Our attention and focus is a muscle we can build.

The Darker Side of Distraction

Distraction can be defeated by consistently applying the first principle we learned – The Power of 'No'. But when this unbridled assault on our attention leads to stress and anxiety, that's a whole other ballgame with more dangerous consequences for our health and well-being.

For the purposes of this book let's just say that this stress and the negative outlook that inevitably flows from it are absolute productivity killers! So, we need to find ways of increasing productivity while reducing stress. To do this, we use tools that increase our positivity and increase our attention to the present moment, rather than allowing us to be debilitated by the way our minds are prone to dwell on the failures of the past or fears of the future.

As I became more senior and responsible for more people I had to learn how not to waste energy worrying because it reduced my concentration, my creativity and ultimately my productivity. I began to experiment with tools and strategies that not only reshaped my inner monologue but also built up my concentration – I've included some of them in the application section below.

The Spirit - Emotional Energy

A deficit of physical and mental energy can produce negative stress, but they can also impact our emotional energy. When we suffer this, we can quickly become irritable and impatient, or anxious and insecure. Such states of emotional energy deficit cause friction in our work and social relationships, reducing team effectiveness. They also often negatively impact the way clients respond to us as well, which can rapidly affect the bottom line!

Having said that, by far the most significant wellspring of emotional energy is your spirit. Emotional Energy comes from the extent to which your daily activities are aligned with your core values and the degree to which you experience a sense of meaning and purpose.

Given the relentless assault on our attention and the typical deficits in both our physical and mental energy reserves, it's no wonder that many people don't even consider that these are perhaps the most powerful sources of energy, that they are in fact the catalysts for profound focus, perseverance, and resilience. That they are fundamental to unlocking more productivity.

The key is making space to recognize what your values are and what provides you with a sense of meaning and purpose in the first place. Then you need to identify those tasks and activities that are aligned with your values and that fuel your sense of meaning and purpose and do more of them.

The trouble is, not many people make the time to do this, not many people decide this is important enough to invest in. The most common mistake organizations and individuals make is to think this is solely about happiness or fulfillment. In doing so, they miss out on accessing a tremendous amount of emotional energy that fuels massive productivity.

In the first 10 years of my career, I learned to manage some elements of physical and mental energy. I didn't really manage my emotional energy very well, and I had some very painful experiences because of that. I made sure that physically I was in good shape because that's what you're supposed to do. All the books on focus and productivity tell you physically you've got to be in good shape. I ran, I went to the gym, I rowed, and I did lots of things to keep my body relatively well-tuned. (I didn't really recognize the role food played till much later.) My faith provided some renewal for my emotional energy, but I was ignoring it for the most part. But what I didn't understand was the toll that took on my emotional energy, the reserves I was depleting in resilience or patience. I moved from being somebody who was very calm, very considered, to someone who became more reactive and more emotional, more often depressed. I wasn't charging my emotional batteries; I wasn't building-in time to recharge and restore emotionally.

I hadn't learned the true benefits of aligning my activities with my values or discovering more deeply what gave me meaning and purpose. But when I did, the energy that was available for me to help somebody, for me to take a business decision, for me to stay up all night looking after my sick children, was available to me much more easily. There was simply more energy available in all three realms. That's why I now manage energy and not time.

Implementing just some of the tools in this chapter will help you unlock more energy more quickly than I did! They will ultimately Unlock a More Productive You!

APPLICATION

Tools to increase:

Physical Energy
Mental Energy
Emotional Energy

Physical Energy
Tool 1 - Manage the sprint not the marathon
One particular counter-intuitive strategy I regularly use and get clients to use is to take breaks at more frequent yet specific intervals – to unplug and completely disengage for brief periods. The rationale behind this is to leverage Ultradian rhythms. Ultradian rhythms are 90 to 120-minute cycles during which our bodies slowly move from a high-energy state into a physiological trough. Toward the end of each cycle, the body begins to crave a period of recovery.

Without this recovery we begin to experience physical restlessness, yawning, hunger, and difficulty concentrating, but many of us ignore them and keep working. Our capacity to focus, our patience and our resilience all begin to be diminished. Intermittent breaks result in higher and more sustainable performance. So make sure you plan them into your schedule!

Tool 2 - Manage your Sleep-lag!

Another issue that commonly needs to be addressed is sleep, both its quality and quantity. Do you accomplish more in three hours when you're sleep-deprived or in one hour when you feel energetic, optimistic and engaged?

Circadian rhythms are physiological cycles within a 24hr period that we each have - essentially our body clock. Typically, high-performers and passionate entrepreneurs ignore and override these natural rhythms and then wonder why they can't sleep or can't sleep well.

So instead, pay attention to and learn how to synchronize activities with your own internal signals for sleeping and waking. This will have huge energy benefits and typically lead to significant increases in performance. One simple strategy to effect massive change in your sleep cycle is to change when your alarm goes off. Don't set your alarm for when you want to wake up, instead set it to remind you to go to sleep!

When this alarm goes off, finish up any work on your computer, turn off the TV, check your social media for the last time, turn off any unnecessary lights and do something calm like reading, meditation, praying, reflecting on your day and being grateful.

Sleep experts recommend that to get the optimal sleep you should start an evening wind-down routine about an hour before you intend to sleep. Try it for 5 nights in a row and see how just how refreshed, reinvigorated and restored you feel by the time you hit the weekend!

Tool 3 – Avoid GIGO

I love this old programming acronym: Garbage In, Garbage Out. It's particularly true when it comes to nutrition - I could go into a lot of detail around how different diets affect energy levels and moods for people. But learning and then addressing your own unique nutritional need is what makes all the difference. And it's not just what you eat but when you eat too.

For me, while I remained pretty fit for most of my career, I hadn't focused too much on my diet. One New Years Eve, we were having a party, and there was a nutritionist from L.A. who was at our house. I'd just eaten something, and I immediately became utterly fatigued. I thought it was just the wine and being exhausted after a hard week and my body had just reacted to the permission I'd given myself to relax.

But this nutritionist had spotted something. She'd noticed some other physiological symptoms I was displaying too. So she took me through a 21 indicator survey and identified that I had a gluten intolerance. I completely reshaped my diet over the course of the following year. I then began experimenting, figuring out what foods catalyzed what response from my body, mind, and emotions. Certain foods and combinations of food were impacting how much focus and patience I had throughout a day. Other foods were impacting how I felt when I woke up in the morning and how quickly I could spin-up my enthusiasm and be on point for the day.

That was an object lesson for me. That first 72 hours was a revelation; going from not really worrying about my diet, to taking gluten out of my diet. And when I did the transformation was remarkable: I had increased energy, I had increased concentration, I had better control of my emotions. Pasta, bread, certain types of rice, cereals, you name it all had to go, but the payoff was worth it for me.

Nutrition is incredibly personal though as everyone's physiologies are different. First, get some consistency into when you eat, then see a nutritionist or a functional medicine practitioner, take an intolerance test – try some new diets – and find out just how much better you can feel!

And here's something you can do without the cost and without taking up too much time if you need some encouragement to increase your motivation and will power around your food choices – ask yourself: "What would Batman eat?" And yes I am being serious.

Studies by Professor Brian Wansink at Cornell University have shown that when kids asked themselves this question before eating they are more likely to reach for apple slices over french fries. I guess you think this might only work for kids… but you would be wrong.

In his super practical book, "Slim by Design: Mindless Eating Solutions for Everyday Life" Brian explains:

"The same thing works for adults. If you're faced with a decision like, "Should I eat dessert?" think of an admired person in your life. Say to yourself, "What would my cool friend Steve do?" You'll find that about a third of the time it will be easier for you to make healthier decisions."

Mental Energy

Tool 4 – Control your environment

Increasing focus isn't just an exercise in will power; it isn't just a stronger application of the Power of 'No,' it's a smarter one. Control over your environment is crucial to the amount of mental energy you can access or recharge. Invariably, the most productive people exercise more control over where, when and how they work than those who are less productive.

Tim Ferris, productivity guru and author of "The 4 Hour Work Week" explains that:

"Focus is a function, first and foremost, of limiting the number of options you give yourself for procrastinating... I think that focus is thought of this magical ability. It's not a magical ability. It's put yourself in a padded room, with the problem that you need to work on, and shut the door. That's it. The degree to which you can replicate that, and systematize it, is the extent to which you will have focus."

So, conference room, Starbucks, notifications switched off, voicemail on, whatever is your version of controlling the stimulus that would otherwise tempt you to break your focus, just remove it.

Tool 5 – Make space in your head

If something is important, write it down, don't keep thinking about it. If something is worrying you, write it down, don't keep thinking about it. Unresolved issues in your world don't just distract you they reduce your intelligence! Cal Newport calls this "attention residue."

The solution is to get the things out of your head by writing them down. Why does this work? Neuroscientist Daniel J. Levitin explains that writing things down deactivates "rehearsal loops" in your brain:

"When we have something on our minds that is important – especially a To Do Item – we're afraid we'll forget it, so our brain rehearses it, tossing it around and around in circles in something that cognitive scientists actually refer to as the rehearsal loop, a network of brain regions that ties together the frontal cortex just behind your eyeballs and the hippocampus in the center of your brain... The problem is that it works too well, keeping the item in rehearsal until we attend to them. Writing them down gives both implicit and explicit permission to the rehearsal loop to let them go, to relax its neural circuits so that we can focus on something else."

Then write down an answer to the following question in relation to everything you've written down:

"What action will I take to address this thing that is on my mind and when?"

Tool 6 – Don't multitask

There isn't a complicated way of saying this. Research shows that our brains are not very good at multitasking. We think we can, but we can't. We try, and then we wonder why we are not productive. Do one thing at a time, well. If you read the last chapter you know, we talked about the tax of 'Context Switching.' It's real, but its cure is simple. Don't do it. Do one thing at a time.

There, now you don't have to read Gary Keller's book "One Thing" – but if you want to know more, do.

Tool 7 – Meditate

If you want to improve your concentration, this is weightlifting for your attention span. Not only does meditation and mindfulness practice reduce stress, combat depression and increase happiness, studies have shown that regular meditation can help people focus their attention and sustain it.

I'm not suggesting you become a monk or schedule a few hours of intense meditation each day. Rather, the benefits of meditation can be had from as little a 2-5 minutes each day. However, if you want to undertake more significant brain training and re-programming, then a recent study at Massachusetts General Hospital showed that practicing meditation for 27 minutes a day created lasting brain changes in 8 weeks.

Emotional Energy
Tool 8 - Improve your Outlook

Dr. Seligman and his team at Princeton and subsequently Penn University discovered that your outlook is determined by your explanation style - how you explain an event that happens to yourself in your own mind.

If you change this explanation style, you can change your outlook! Basically, you can re-program your mind for sustained optimism, which in turn combats the stress related mental energy deficits, which in turn makes you more productive.

Here's a quick tool to do just that:

Before you go to sleep tonight open your "notes app" on your phone or better still, go find a pen and paper -

Then write a list of 3 things that were good today.

They don't have to be super significant or the most incredible thing ever, just that you thought they were good

–   "I finished my report on time."

–   "My husband picked up my favorite ice cream for dessert on the way home from work today."

–   "My sister just got a positive report on her health after the cancer scare."

Next, to each of the 3 things, answer the question - "Why did this happen?"

For example, if you listed finishing your report...

you might write down that it was because "My team really pulled together and got me the content I needed" or because "I wanted it done so I could enjoy the weekend with my kids for a change!".

If you wrote down that your husband picked up ice cream...

you might write "because my husband is really thoughtful sometimes" or "because I remembered to call him from work and remind him to stop by the grocery store."

Or if you thought about, your sister's positive report on her health...

you might say it was because "God was looking out for her" or "She did everything her physicians asked of her."

Did you notice that the strategy didn't try to re-interpret a negative event it is simply a conscious choice to spend some time deliberately finding and then focusing on what went well today and a positive explanation for it - the more we do this, the more we interrupt the constant flow of negative explanations.

Research shows that just one week of doing this results in a slight shift in our explanation style, being less-depressed, happier and with increased mental capacity, increased mental bandwidth!

Tool 9 – Be more of who you are

Do more of what you do best and enjoy most at work;

Consciously allocate time and energy to the areas of your life - work, family, health, service to others - you deem most important; and live your core values in your daily behaviors.

I've already given you 2 helpful Tools in the previous chapter, but here are 2 additional strategies you can use to help you implement this in more detail in your schedule.

Strategy - What Matters Most

Step 1. Don't do this exercise today –

Instead, schedule a 15-minute space in an upcoming day when you're going to do it. Write it in your calendar with a 15-minute margin either side to give you some wiggle room.

Make sure your schedule is synced and you and the person who most impacts your schedule know about this protected time

...so they can encourage you to make sure it happens. Now get on with your day/week and forget about this for the time being.

Step 2. When the day has arrived, and it's now time to do this
  –   start your 15-minute session by taking 8 full breaths...
  –   concentrating solely on those breaths...

When you've taken your 8 breaths, start a timer for 3 minutes and reflect on this question – just think, don't do anything else -

"What handful of activities are responsible for the disproportionate number of your successes – the times when you feel good or when you don't care how long it takes you to do something?"

When the timer is done, write a few short sentences about what came up.

Step 3. Now set your timer for another 3 minutes but don't start it yet - take another 8 breaths – then, set your timer going while you reflect on this second question – again, just think, don't do anything else:

"What handful of activities absolutely bomb your productivity – what drains your energy or leaves you feeling empty?"

When the timer is done write a few short sentences about what came up.

Step 4. Now spend 3 minutes examining your schedule for the previous day; what you did and when, yesterday....

Retrospectively, where could you have made modifications to your schedule to do more of the things uncovered by answering the first question I posed?

and then answer this question:

"Where could you have eliminated some of the things you identified in response to the second question?"

Not only have you identified things that are good for you and what matters to you, you've already figured out what you could have done differently in a day you've already lived.

The trick is to implement this now going forward...

Strategy – Making space

So let's take a look at a technique for making important things happen in the future

- in a day that has yet to happen

- no matter how busy you are or how much inertia you suffer from...

Step 1. Let's start by thinking about tomorrow.

From the mental or physical list of things you have to do and want to do tomorrow, identify your 2 most important todo's for the entire day.

What works best for me is to do this before my evening meal, when I'm closing out work for the day, but what I emphasize to clients is that no matter when they choose to do it, it always has to be done in advance of the next day – not the same day.

Step 2. Once you've identified your 2 most important todo's, schedule when - and be specific here - in your upcoming day, you are going to do those 2 most important tasks – the ones that will most contribute to how fulfilled you are in that day.

Make sure you create a margin of 15 minutes either side to give you some protected space. Once that's done – put it away and get on with your evening or other tasks you need to get done.

Step 3. Now during that following day and 5 minutes before the time you specified for the first of your two most important tasks, set a 5-minute countdown timer.

This gives you a window to shut down your distractions, especially email and texts – and then the moment it pings you're up –

...now is your most important time to focus on your day, and you, your subconscious and your environment are primed to get it done.

Step 4. Put your phone at least 10 feet away from you on silent or, better still, give it to someone else who you've instructed not to give it back to you until you've finished – and that's it.

Studies have shown that you are far less likely to procrastinate or stall if you've
- planned a day ahead
- been specific as to the exact time

- given yourself the flexibility of a 15-minute grace period
- experienced the anticipation of a countdown to start; and
- reduced the distraction of email, text, twitter and facebook notifications.

These two simple strategies will enable you to begin to access more Emotional Energy by experiencing more fulfillment, feeling more purposeful and doing more of what matters to you – getting more done of what is truly important to you.

CHAPTER 11

Harness Ritual And Routine: Don't Be A Slave To Them

You now know why and on what to use your 'No' if you want to be more productive.

You now know what to do to conserve, increase and access more energy to be more productive.

It's great to know these things, but you have to actually do them. So, now you need a system to make it easier to implement these core principles day in and day out so that you Unlock a More Productive You!

It seems counterintuitive at first, but the key to getting things done is to make them more automatic.

What are we doing when we automate something in business? We are trying to achieve two things:

•   freeing up resources so that those resources can be used more effectively for other, more important, things; and

•   creating a process to deliver consistent results, to make sure the success is replicated over and over again.

The same is true for our own personal productivity - the resource is willpower, and the process is ritual and routine. The key to unlocking both is by leveraging existing habits and forming new ones – harnessing ritual and routine.

Asleep at the wheel

Have you ever had that experience where you woke up, had breakfast and then suddenly realized you're in work and you didn't remember the subway journey there or the route your drove that morning?

I remember having that experience during my training contract in a town called Sheffield. I was at my desk and I couldn't remember how I'd gotten there. I had somehow done this 25-minute cross-town drive, parked my car and walked up the stairs to the floor where my office was and not noticed a single turn or stop light on the way in. It was a miracle I made it to my desk safely!

How the mind operates once you get into this space called habit, is amazing. Numerous studies have shown that when you are acting out of habit, brain activity dips. It is almost as if you're asleep. Now, you're not asleep; you're still functioning. The nervous system is still taking in all these signals that I talked about when I was talking about the genetic basis of the Power of 'No', but you're not fully conscious of all the complicated steps that are involved in the habitual behavior. The motor skills that are required, the muscle memory, the simple cognition, all of these are set to automatic, and you just aren't conscious of it - like me driving to work, not quite asleep at the wheel, but certainly not making conscious decisions.

Willpower

Willpower fuels our conscious decisions. Willpower is like a rechargeable battery for most people: once it's been used up, it needs recharging.

So if you're going to exercise your 'no' more effectively and if you want to positively change the behaviors that most impact your energy, then you are going to need discipline and self-control, you're going to need willpower.

Our willpower gets progressively depleted throughout the day by every conscious choice we make. However, the simple fact is this: anything you can set to do automatically, anything that we can do habitually or as a ritual or within a set routine, doesn't tax your limited supply of willpower.

"It is a profoundly erroneous truism that we should cultivate the habit of thinking of what we are doing. The precise opposite is the case. Civilization advances by extending the number of operations we can perform without thinking about them" – AN Whitehead 1911

Rituals help us perform actions without thinking about them.

Rituals

So what are rituals? Well, they are highly specific behaviors, done at precise times, so that they eventually become automatic and no longer require conscious will or discipline.

The most effective role for your pre-frontal cortex - your mind's center for reason, logic, problem-solving and planning - is to decide what behavior you want to change, design the ritual you'll undertake, and then get out of the way.

You may have identified some of your existing rituals when you were examining your behavior throughout the day in the last chapter to determine your energy usage. Certainly, rituals can be intermittent breaks throughout your day - picking up a book between tasks and reading a chapter, going for a 20-minute walk after you've eaten lunch. Many high-performing athletes have pre-game rituals that they use to get into the zone.

These Rituals get internalized through habit.

Your habits don't have to be your kryptonite

I love Charles Duhigg – he is an award-winning New York Times reporter who writes extensively on the power of habit. His perspective on the scientific discoveries that explain why habits exist and how they can be changed is profound. I have been able to reshape and harness my habits and help many of my clients re-shape theirs because of his insight and the tools and strategies I've learned to apply them.

Essentially there are three sequential elements to a habit:

1.   The cue - which starts off right at the beginning and is what triggers you, in effect, to undertake a certain kind of behavior.

2.   The behavior itself - the thing that you do, whether that be smoking, reaching for that extra cookie, reactively checking instafacetwitchat the moment you hear a ping, instinctively grabbing the glass of wine at 5:30, sitting on the sofa flicking on the TV every night, putting off that report (procrastination is a habit); and then

3.   The reward - the reward you get for the behaviors listed above. It might be a sense of security, the comfort, the endorphin hit from having a cigarette, whatever it is, that comes from the behavior.

The research shows that by identifying the true reward and altering the routine you use to get it without messing with the cue, you can learn to interrupt and reprogram the habit. Trying to simply stop the behavior without addressing the reward is, in most cases, futile.

Forming a new habit relies on creating a new cue and reward system to shape the routine. Like the visual cue of putting your trainers by the side of your bed - untied and ready to go - that triggers your prospective memory (the remembrance of the future you want in this case you running) to help you develop the habit of running in the morning.

You need to make sure that you give yourself either an immediate small reward or a reminder of the ultimate reward that this new habit of running is going to give you. For example, if you like peanut butter, reward yourself with a small spoonful of the best peanut butter you can buy immediately you have come in from your run! A reminder of the ultimate reward could be buying the suit you want to get into for the awards ceremony you're going to attend and hanging it on your bedroom door, fixing a post-it note on your mirror or refrigerator door with the number on the scale you want to weigh by the end of that month, etc.

I used this exact method when I had just qualified as an attorney and wanted to cycle to work instead of driving. My goal was so that I could be mentally focused longer in the day by keeping in peak physical shape. I wanted to get my exercise in without impacting my 6-Minute-Units and by using what I thought would otherwise be unproductive time – driving in rush hour traffic. In my case it was cycling shoes by the bed – I never went so far as some people do in wearing their training clothes to bed though!

But aren't we supposed to be more mindful?

As I've been writing this chapter I've been working with a client looking to address habits around maintaining her wellness. She feels these habits are negative and interfering with the growth of her business. We've been exploring the tools and strategies unique to her and looking at her rituals and routines. The interesting thing was that when we first talked about this, the words "ritual" and "routine" had such negative connotations for her.

Using the word ritual triggered a memory for her of phrases like "Oh, you just do that out of ritual." 'But routine, its unconscious", "Ritual is mindless" and one of my favorites; "I thought you were teaching me how to be more mindful!"

For many people something that is done by ritual or out of routine equals being boring, being dull, or something you have begun to do without thinking.

In fact, it's just the opposite. When we harness the power of habit to create a ritual then we use up less conscious decision-making energy, we use less willpower. Why? So that we can use it for things that really matter.

Tim Ferris puts it like this: "I encourage people to develop routines so that their decision-making is only applied to the most creative aspects of their work, or wherever their unique talent happens to lie."

And when you create a ritual that is pregnant with meaning for you, when the cues you create are important to some significant goal or something you want to achieve, the ritual is way, way more powerful.

Most habits have been adopted unconsciously. Most rituals are adopted through peer pressure and crowd dynamics, not conscious decision. That's why they are often derided and looked down upon. Many people are slaves to their habits, ignorant of why they adopted certain rituals in the first place and locked into a routine that doesn't serve them.

Harnessing ritual and routine

But, forming a habit deliberately, creating a ritual to achieve a particular purpose, setting up a routine to achieve a specific goal is the opposite of being mindless. The ritual or habit becomes a tool, a success system.

Athletes can teach us something here. In their New York Times bestseller: "The Power of Full Engagement", Jim Loehr, and Tony Schwartz state:

"At a practical level, they build very precise routines for managing energy in all spheres of their lives – eating and sleeping; working out and resting; summoning appropriate emotions; mentally preparing and staying focused, and regularly connecting to the mission they have set for themselves. Although most of us spend little or no time systematically training in any of these dimensions, we are expected to perform at our best for eight, ten and even twelve hours a day."

Not merely a battery, more like a muscle

Although I've said willpower is like a battery and needs to be recharged when it gets used up, it is also like a muscle, the more you use it, the stronger it grows.

Research shows that people who use their willpower to create habits and routines in one area of their lives, regularly find that they can exercise more self-control and discipline in all areas of their lives – thus compounding their effectiveness.

So how can you harness ritual and routine to Unlock a More Productive You? How can you adopt a system of success?

APPLICATION

Managing Willpower

Tool 1 – Use Willpower to Build Willpower

Just a little bit of practice every day can increase self-control and improving self-control in one area tends to improve all areas – so find something small you can practice with.

Tool 2 - Plan your reaction ahead of time

Decide ahead of time how you will respond when your willpower is going to be taxed in a given situation. The evidence shows that you are more likely to adopt the response you planned if you have chosen it in advance. Maybe use an "If this then that" framework to help you:

- If I am offered ice cream or cake at work, then I will say, "thank you but I'm allergic."
- If I wake up and my alarm goes off at 7 AM, then I will get out of bed immediately and go for a 15-minute walk.
- If I get hungry in between meals, then I will go get a big glass of water and walk around the office.
- If I come home from work, then I will immediately go exercise before sitting down on the couch to watch TV.
- If I plan on losing weight, then I will only eat THESE foods and not anything else.

Tool 3 – Conserve your decision-making energy

Reducing the number and difficulty of decisions in your day is an easy way to conserve energy. Planning ahead for when you will consider and make decisions is a start and so is harnessing ritual and routine for the less important ones.

Tool 4 – Eat

Snack, but snack healthily. Studies show that we tend to make poor decisions when our metabolism is low – we've already talked about your Ultradian rhythm, so get to know yours and anticipate when your energy will dip. Then take a break and eat a small, healthy, snack. This will help you replenish willpower quickly.

Tool 5 - Use a pre-commitment device

Asking your significant other in advance not to let you eat dessert at the restaurant you're going to later in the evening is an example of a pre-commitment device. Why not increase its effectiveness by adding incentive and risk into the mix: Give a friend 500 dollars and tell them they can keep it if you don't follow through on a particular goal.

Tool 6 – Manage your environment

Again, we briefly touched on this in the last chapter, but one of the most powerful ways to change your behavior is merely choosing the right environment. If you have a spot where you are usually productive, go there repeatedly. According to Prof. Wendy Wood of USC, your environment activates habits without your conscious mind ever noticing. Hence why it is less of a drain on willpower and can even increase. It can also have the added side effect of removing you from distractions and interruptions!

Changing and Creating Habits
Tool 7 – Changing an existing Habit

Identify the cue that spurs it on – Is it the time of day? Boredom? Hunger? Stress?

Identify the potential rewards – Happiness? Energy? Satisfaction?

Identify a new routine you'd like to establish that results in the same 'reward' from the negative behavior...but in a more productive and healthy way.

For example: Maybe you want to stop eating multiple energy and protein bars between meals all day long, and you feel like you need them to get through the day, but it's leading to weight gain.

IDENTIFY THE CUE AND REWARD: Make a note in a notebook every time you're hungry, and identify a cue and reward. Test out different routines that lead you to a healthier (yet still desired) reward:

• If you're bored or lack energy, maybe it's push-ups or a shot of espresso.

• If you're burned out from work, maybe it's 5 minutes spent watching cute French Bulldogs on Instagram.

• If it's lack of socialization, maybe it's walking over to your friend's desk WITHOUT opening the can of soda.

BUILD THE NEW ROUTINE: Try out different things, and then write down your results. Which ones still gave you the happy feeling of eating without eating unhealthy foods. Once you've identified the cue that's causing your bad habit, add a new routine that still gives you the desired results.

Tool 8 – Forming a new Habit

Maybe you want to create a new morning routine that enables you to get up 10 minutes earlier rather than being thrust headlong into the madness of the day.

• Create a cue, a new trigger in the morning to program the new routine. Maybe use a different alarm sound for a change, maybe change the brand of coffee, maybe lay your clothes out for the day ahead of time or even your sneakers for a morning run.

• Choose the reward. What is it that you get? Maybe it's the opportunity to savor your first espresso uninterrupted by the kids. Maybe it will be the additional focus you get, from having a few moments of peace to be still in the morning. Or maybe it will be the capacity to smile more at your kids when they bounce into your room. Whatever it is, make a conscious decision to recognize it and choose that.

Again, try a few things and write down your results. Establish which ones make it easier and then find ways of reinforcing those.

Harnessing Ritual and Routine

I don't know of a single productive person who doesn't use a process, have a ritual or follow a routine to get their results. As we've already identified these processes, rituals and routines reduce the tax on our willpower. They work because they make things automatic, they take away the energetic cost of conscious decision-making.

When you have chosen them, routines and rituals have the added advantage that they help you feel in control and non-reactive, which reduces anxiety and increases productivity.

If you are like many of my clients, you have probably adopted your morning and evening rituals and routines and by default. They weren't consciously designed by you. I've found that making small adjustments to either can significantly increase productivity. However, if you want to effect a step-change in your productivity then re-designing and implementing entirely new rituals and routines are the way to go.

Routines

You need to know your existing patterns - the preprogrammed routines and the rituals you've adopted – so that you can plan more effectively how and what to change. We're so often oblivious to them, and this self-knowledge exercise alone is often enough to shake things up for the people I work with.

Tool 9 – Design your new morning Routine

So, you need to monitor and record in a notebook everything you do for the first 90 minutes of your day. Do this for five days in a row, which will give you a good overall perspective. And you'll see that you already have patterns in place. Okay now you've done that, what should you change and what do you want to change in order to be more have more focus and energy throughout the day to be more productive?

Here are few suggestions from my morning routine:
- Wake up early - to get ahead of the madness
- Don't check your phone for the first 45 minutes of your day
- Be still – even if it just for 2-3 minutes – doing nothing or, if it works for you, meditating
- Say some affirmations – statements that remind you of who you are and where you're going

- Express Gratitude – there's an incredible amount of research on the benefits of this simple practice
- Get active – whether it's yoga, running or simply walking around the block – the effects are incredibly positive and the time spent doesn't have to be extensive either – why not try a 7-minute workout?

If you don't do anything else from this Chapter implement this one thing to increase your productivity immediately!

Don't check your phone first thing in the morning

Your phone is one of the most significant sources of stress in the morning. When a message comes in in the morning and you immediately look at it you're setting yourself up to react to someone else's goals. You are permitting them to direct your attention. You are not prioritizing and planning your own day; you're allowing your objectives to be hijacked by whoever randomly decides to enter your phone. So, don't do it – instead, give yourself a 45-minute phone sabbatical at the start of each day (better 90 minutes if you can manage it).

You may be one of the many people have trained themselves to wake up in the state of fight or flight - having an elevated cortisol level (the stress hormone). You may have unintentionally programmed this response by your repeated experience of low-level anxiety about what your phone is going to demand of you the moment you wake up - so why don't you try not giving it that power over you? Just 5 days of this simple practice can reduce your morning cortisol levels.

Transform your Schedule into a 'Success System'

Your schedule is your most important productivity tool for enforcing your 'no' and managing your energy. It also helps you establish routines by managing both your own and others' expectations of you and commits you to specific time slots, which improves self-discipline.

Knowing how to make it work for you is crucial to Unlocking a More Productive You!

Tool 10 – Challenge your Schedule

One of the most powerful thoughts on productivity that I was introduced to, was by Stephen Covey: "The key is not to prioritize your schedule, but to schedule your priorities." This was the catalyst for me to first challenge my schedule and make it work for me rather than me serving it.

Your schedule should be a personal 'Success System' – to begin to develop an overarching principle for your system, do these three things:

• Answer the question: "What handful of activities are responsible for the disproportionate number of your successes – the times when you feel good or when you don't care how long it takes you to do something?"

• Answer the question: "What handful of activities absolutely bomb your productivity – what drains your energy or leaves you feeling empty?"

• Arrange your schedule to do more of #1 and less of #2.

And don't forget, before entering anything into your schedule, always ask the most powerful question of all: "Do I need to do this at all?"

Tool 11 – Schedule your deep work

You need to know the difference between your deep work and your shallow work. Here's Cal Newport again:

"Shallow work is little stuff like email, meetings, moving information around. Things that are not really using your talents. Deep work pushes your current abilities to the limits. It produces high-value results and improves your skills."

So use your schedule to plan when you'll do your most difficult tasks, the ones that tax your concentration the most, the ones that bring the highest value results. These can be done in your peak hours when your energy is highest. For me, these tasks are researching and writing and my peak hours are between 8 and 11, surprisingly both morning and evening! I schedule-in these activities in 3 blocks across my week to make sure I commit 9 hours to growing.

Tool 12 – Schedule your priorities

To schedule them, you have to know your priorities. You should have gotten a good sense of your longer-term priorities by now from the tools in the previous chapters. But the daily and weekly planning cycles need a slightly more refined focus. Each day you may have 2-3 of activities that you must get to.

If they are not recurring activities, identify them at the close of the previous day or first thing each morning and lock them into your peak hours – allowing a good margin either side of the time you allocated – we nearly always undershoot by overestimating our work rate!

Tool 13 - Schedule your emails

Specifically, plan when you will read your emails in batches – some of the highest performers only check email 3 times per day. First, in the office immediately following their peak hours, second, immediately after lunch and third about 45 minutes before their close down ritual.

Use your schedule to create a routine that others recognize and respect, and you stick to.

Adopt a close-down ritual
Tool 14 – Schedule your close down

Choose in advance a time to stop work. Yes, I did say that. It is a consistent feature of the highest performers and is the signature of some of the most productive people I know. It is one of the most important transitions in my day – usually it signals time to cook, one of my new-found loves!

Adopting a close down ritual gives you a target for the day, forces you to align your schedule and the activities within it to a specific end point. It also forces you to anticipate how long each of your activities and tasks might take and estimate more precisely much you can fit in your schedule.

Block out the last 45 minutes of your day for two main tasks:
- Determining your priorities for tomorrow; and
- Reflecting on the learning from the day.

The first releases background mental energy and also allows you to relax more deeply for your evening, which in turn improves your sleep.

The second has been shown to improve productivity by as much as 22% just by itself.

Establish a wind-down routine

It's fitting that I end with the benefits of a wind-down routine and particularly one that increases your chance of getting a good night's sleep. There is not a single expert that doesn't highlight the role of sleep on productivity.

To sum up a wealth of research, if you don't get enough quality sleep (unaided by pharmaceuticals!) then your willpower will be depleted, self-control will be reduced, you're more likely to adopt bad habits, your relationships will suffer, and your intelligence will decrease in certain circumstances.

Tool 15 – Avoid screen time 45 minutes before sleep

Sleep hygienists know that - the evidence is overwhelming that - you will fall asleep more quickly without any medicinal help, drugs or what have you, and you will sleep for longer in a deep sleep, not REM sleep if you turn your screens off 45 minutes or more before you put your head on your pillow.

In our Circadian rhythms, alternately sleep inducing or waking hormones are triggered in our brain based on light sensitivity. Our screens (phones, tablets, and our TVs) emit a particular frequency of light that tells our brain it's time to wake up, so if you're trying to have a good night's sleep avoid screen time for at least 45 minutes before you sleep.

But to be able to do that, you need to create a new routine, a new habit for the evening, and you need to create cues, your own ritual, in order to implement them.

Your own routine

Again, you need to know your existing patterns - the preprogrammed routines and the rituals you've adopted – so that you can plan more effectively how and what to change.

Monitor and record what you do 5 nights in a row – ask yourself these questions:

"What am I doing every night?"

Am I consistent on when I walk into the bathroom I brush my teeth?

Am I consistent in making that cup of tea or coffee?

Do I watch TV in my bedroom and then turn it out?

Do I read?

Is the last thing that I do check FaceBook to stoke my FOMO?"

When I recommend to clients that they avoid screen time at the end of the day, they often ask

"What am I going to do for those 45 minutes?"

Well, there are some positive things you can incorporate into a ritual that will become reinforced by habit that will ultimately help you Unlock a More Productive You!

Here are a few that people have found time for and incorporated into their wind down routine:

- Assess the day – what did you learn? What did you contribute?
- Acknowledge the successes of the day, recognize the small wins
- Reflect upon the connections you made
- Express gratitude
- Determine your priorities for tomorrow
- Choose your clothes for the next day
- Read the books you never had time for
- Do something calming or soothing like taking a bath or lighting some incense
- Review the day with your significant other

You'll suddenly a) create space, b) improve your ability to sleep more soundly, c) connect more deeply with your partner and d) ensure surprises for the following day are minimized.

Afterword

I've said it a few times in this book, the issue is not more time – the real issue is space to focus, energy to get things done and a system to make sure it happens consistently.

That's what I've endeavored to do in writing this book; to give you 3 Keys to enable you to create space to focus, increase your energy to get things done and adopt a system to make sure you can do it over and over again.

If you trust the tools and do the work then you will *Unlock a More Productive You!* That's my desire for you, for you to get more done, of what matters most. And to do that without the stress, overwhelm and anxiety that our hyper-connected, always-on, intensely demanding world provokes in us! This book will help you do that.

I'm grateful to the many teachers I've had – some of their lessons I learned quickly, many more took a long time for me to recognize and even longer to put into practice.

Your success doesn't have to come at the expense of your health and your most valuable relationships. I made many mistakes that you don't have to. I paid a price to learn these things that you don't have to pay.

If you'd like to go deeper in learning how to *Unlock a More Productive You!* then I'd love to see you at one of my seminars, workshops or masterclasses. Visit www.charliehughjones.com and sign up to be the first to know about FREE Training, Videos,

Webinars, New Publications, Speaking Engagements, Events and so much more. I'd love to keep in touch.

If you'd like to work with me as your coach, to help keep you accountable for your own transformation, and to help you Unlock the Best Version of You! then please reach out to me by emailing charliehughjones@mac.com to see if you qualify to work with me directly.

Here's to the Best Version of You,
Charlie

ABOUT THE AUTHOR

From his working class roots in an industrial northern town in England, Charlie Hugh-Jones achieved his goal of becoming the youngest partner in a top national law firm within 10 years of leaving college. Just nine months after making partner Charlie left his high profile legal career to start his first successful business - helping organizations and individuals achieve their goals faster.

Over the last 15 years he has worked with:
• Fortune 500 companies/global brands
• Governments/healthcare systems
• Technology start-ups, and

- the high-performing leaders that run these organizations

Helping them clarify their goals, develop effective strategies to meet their objectives and then take positive action to deliver on them.

Charlie suffered a number of tragedies along the way that included personal and professional betrayal, failure and loss. The tools, techniques and strategies he learned to re-build his life and serve others more effectively are now the authentic foundation of his clients' success.

As a father of 4 and married to the most incredible woman, Charlie lives 200 yards from the Ocean in Florida and writes, speaks and coaches all over the world on how to Unlock the Best Version of You!